N3

UNDERSTANDING
LIFE

COVER PICTURE

Deliverance by Brian Exton of www.picturerealm.co.uk

The hand is perhaps a metaphor for the hand of destiny. The size
of the woman in relation to it, is the same scale perhaps, as a
spirit or soul is to the human body.

We will often come on a reconnoitre visit to a planet prior to
incarnation, especially a nursery world, which is the status of
Earth. This seems to be what this image is about. There are
cosmic causeways which spirit use to travel to and from the spirit
realms. These have a 'stargate' on Earth, with a guardian spirit to
monitor arrivals and activate the gate as required.

UNDERSTANDING LIFE

LIFE

ROGER J BURMAN

Quiet Waters Publishing

First published in 2006
Second publication in 2010

British Library Cataloguing in Publication Data

A catalogue record for this book is available from the British
Library

ISBN 978-0-9542047-3-0

Typeset by CityScape Books
www.cityscapebooks.co.uk

Published by Quiet Waters Publishing
15 Jubilee Way, High Dyke, Navenby
Lincoln, LN5 0BF

Printed and bound by CPI Group (UK) Ltd, Croydon, CR0 4YY

CONTENTS

Introduction

Chapter One   Genesis Revisited

Chapter Two   Life Elsewhere

Chapter Three   The Ascent of Man

Chapter Four   Synchronicity

Chapter Five   The Point of Change

Chapter Six   Titanic Revisited

Chapter Seven   Auschwitz and the Search for Meaning

Chapter Eight   The Difference Between Spirituality and Religion

Chapter Nine   The Syllabus of Unconditional Love

INTRODUCTION

You may think it extreme arrogance or huge delusion, to write about the meaning of life. Being in the media spotlight is no guarantee of wisdom, in fact it makes it probably less likely. It is the way of it that nearly all our scientific advances and new philosophy have started out as the work of an unknown individual. Some the world was slow to recognise at first, sometimes only doing so fully after their lifetime. We forget that today's conventional wisdom was once a minority, heretical view in some cases – the sun not going round the Earth, which is not flat, for example.

We think we are flesh and blood, bones and specialised tissue and so on. These are the physical components of the car we drive we call the body. Our real self is an energy-form or spirit. We sit in the car whilst we have a journey we call an incarnation. Spirit lets the mind do most of the driving, but does take over at critical junctions. This is because all journeys are input into a route planner before we set-off, of which the mind is unaware. Many think of life as being biological, with nothing outside of that possible. The reverse is true. Energy life-forms must exist before any biological ones can do so, and whereas a physical life-form is transient and fleeting, the energy life-form is never ending.

In the case of the spirit capable of incarnating as homo sapiens, what is this energy or spirit? It is thought. It is the ability to produce vibrations which give rise to thought obtained by a complex and dense concentration of energy composed of similar material to light. It is the "creation energy" or "God-energy", the energy capable of producing self-awareness and which is consciousness. It exists in different dimensions simultaneously, although when inside a life-form, it has to spend most of the time in a three dimensional physicality. During waking hours this is something of a prison for the soul, but in sleep a soul may leave the body and journey, and communicate with other spirit.

Each spirit has its own unique vibration, which gives it its individuality. That can show through in a person's voice uniqueness and to a certain extent, facial looks.

Is it not absolutely fascinating how a fertilised human egg, barely perceptible to the eye, can turn into a breathtakingly complex physical structure with the intelligence to build a cruise missile or write a musical symphony? This magic explanation is not DNA by itself, but the presence of the spirit or soul from conception to last breath drawn. Our physical body, our intelligence, our creativity and so on, have spirit as their primary source.

On learning I had given up my business and gone to Scotland to live, a friend of ours exclaimed to a mutual friend, "Roger's gone up the mountain to talk to God!" She knew of my interest in spiritual matters and long-held search for meaning. Much of what I describe in this book is so far removed from conventional thought that the contents may well give the impression she was not incorrect!

My partner and I are not unique in our abilities, just that we are older spirit nearing the end of the journey of very many incarnations, a point that everyone will similarly arrive at in time. Not all older spirits choose the bringing of information to their place of incarnation as the vehicle for the particular life lesson it provides, the lesson being love of mankind on the widest base. Having learned most of the aspects of unconditional love throughout the lifetimes, one of the last is to learn to be unconditional enough to send love out to mankind without restriction or classification; quite simply without condition and often without having personal knowledge of the outcome, but to send it for others, not for one's own gratification.

This is a much simplified version of this deep and complex lesson, but it suffices to explain the point of the lesson. Some obtain this lesson by the deliverance of new information to the place of incarnation but there are other ways that this may be experienced too. All important new spiritual information is introduced primarily by high level five spirit although others may build on it after its introduction. There has not been a continuous release of information, but in saying this, it has been more continuous than one may realise; not all of it becomes widespread or is even acknowledged or accepted by the populace. This does not matter, the lesson is achieved by the delivery of it and the effort and struggle to have it reach as many as possible.

My work will not be easily accepted and will be the object of derision by many. There will however be those to whom it does make sense, that it provides the longed for answers without reference to religious dogma or scientific discourse.

I am of course far from being alone in being a writer of spiritual philosophy, but I am aware of inaccuracies and misinterpretations in the work of others. Who am I to claim superiority? I do not. I offer my work and everyone is free to reject it, criticise it or accept it. For some hopefully it will have the ring of truth; it will pass the "does this feel right" test.

The biggest difficulty we all have, intentionally so, is we temporarily forget on our arrival here, all the knowledge we have in our natural spirit state. We lose memory of the life-plan we composed, of our past lives, of the members of our soul group, of our connection with the Source, of what the spiritual journey is, and so on. To repeat one of my metaphors, we cannot have the challenge, frustration and achievement of a crossword puzzle, if we know all the answers to the clues beforehand.

My first three books were a trilogy to explain life-plans, reincarnation and the spiritual journey. This book moves on and looks at some of the bigger picture: how man came into being; how he compares with life elsewhere; how his technology and civilisation were aided from outside; how life is a tightly controlled drama and synchronicity is our clue to spotting it is so.

Whilst I had the ambition of wanting to explain the world plan for the planet, I limit myself here to looking at two world events: the sinking of the *"Titanic"* and the horror of Auschwitz. It is my thesis there are no accidents in life. Everything is the result of a preconceived plan, individually and globally.

It is at times difficult to see the spiritual reasoning behind events, particularly something as unimaginable as the holocaust. I hope my explanation gives comfort and meaning. I am confident there can be no orthodox religious explanation to such a nightmare. This leads me to go on to explain the vast difference between spirituality and religion. I no doubt will now incur the wrath of the religious establishment for the attempt to shake its philosophical foundation.

In chapter nine, I am amazed and humbled to present the complete syllabus of "unconditional love." Or rather a list of headings to indicate how complex this topic is. As any reader of my earlier books will know, the meaning of life is to explore all the many and varied aspects of unconditional love through practical experience. Life-plans are as varied as all the spirits now incarnated, but there will be similarities between many of them, as each of us must experience everything on the syllabus. If you have a burning desire to know your life purpose, and mediumship is not an option, I suggest dowsing to do so. Please remember, part of the challenge for older spirit, is discovering it for ourselves, and your guide may not answer.

The reader will notice my fondness for quoting the films *"The Matrix"* and *"Matrix Reloaded"*. That is because they put so much spiritual philosophy into a visual form. As the character the Oracle says to the main character Neo, "You didn't come here to make the choice. You've already made it. You came here to understand why you made it." She did not reveal his destiny because we have free-will choice, and spiritual growth comes from its exercise. What those lines do however is state a fundamental spiritual truth, that we chose our experiences beforehand.

One of my tasks is to teach that we all have a spiritual age as well as a biological one. Once this is appreciated, it can explain so much, especially the "square peg in a round hole" syndrome. That is the experience of having little in common with those around us at times, whether family or work colleagues. No need for guilt, this is because you chose in your life-plan the experience of being surrounded by spiritually incompatible people. I attempt to illustrate spiritual age differences by using the tragedies of the

9

"Titanic" and Twin Towers.

Finally in chapter five, I discuss something of the significance of the year 2012, known in spirit as The Point of Change. At the time of writing we have had hurricane Katrina in the USA, the earthquake in Kashmir, and talk of the bird flu virus H5N1 reaching Europe. There is a whole catalogue of manmade and natural disasters scheduled to bring the planet to the point of change of thinking and attitudes particularly in the West. It is the equivalent of a healing crisis, the symptoms will worsen before the condition can improve.

As a consequence of these traumatic events, many will earnestly start their search for meaning. This will be aided by the changes in the planets energies coinciding with the period of these world events. It will also be aided by bodily changes in individual energies, new chakras and so on, opening people to greater spiritual awareness. If you are one such person, I humbly hope this book is of help to you, and indeed, you may look no further.

Roger Burman
Nordcaperen
Hull Marina
East Yorkshire
England
October 2005

CHAPTER ONE

GENESIS REVISITED

Now, at the start of a new spiritual cycle, we are at a particularly interesting time in Earth's evolution, looking at the broad sweep of its spiritual history. As such, it is a time to prefer an incarnation.

How far back does our spiritual history go? The type of spirit that is capable of being human first came here around 11,000 years ago. What is the evidence for that? One piece is the invention of agriculture, which took place around 10,000 years ago. It explains why there was such a long period of time when human-like creatures existed, but did not develop agriculture, which was vital in the progression from hunter-gatherer to static communities. All living things contain spirit, but it was not until the arrival of the spirit type of the highest variety (that is the one capable of incarnating as human) that homo sapiens' evolution took off in the explosion of development that has produced modern man. As we know, this has been instantaneous in comparison with geological time, and at lightning speed in comparison with the length of existence of a bipedal intelligent ape-like creature. What can explain this?

THE EVOLUTION OF PLANETS

That highest spirit variety did not arrive until the planet was ready to receive it. This was done at the end of the last Ice Age in so far as the planet's energies needed to be fine-tuned and repaired in preparation. For the billions of years prior to that, the planet had life, but spiritually the life-forms were the lower forms (plant, fish, bird, reptile and mammal). Whilst man is mammal, he is set apart by speech and intelligence.

I have written in previous books, about each person having a life-plan in place before each incarnation, and that a spirit's evolution goes through five levels with seven stages to each level. I have also spoken of planet Earth being the nursery world in the universe; a world comprised mainly of young spirits, and to which older spirits return to complete their experiences, including that of being teachers to the kindergarten spirits.

Planets have a progression in the same way that an individual spirit does. Their progression is, however, completely different in its stages to a spirit journey. Each planet moves through a series of seven stages and there are no levels within these stages, just evolution through one to seven.

The first stage is the structuring of the planet, the creation of landmass and sea for instance in the case of Earth, and at this very early point, the setting up of the infrastructure of energy lines and rivers (more on these in the next chapter). The second stage includes a settling period during which the planet may host visiting life-forms. The third stage is that of Nursery World. This may be thought of by some as the first level, because it is the first time a planet supports the life-form it is created for, but it is in reality, the third stage for the actual planet.

The stages four through seven correspond roughly to the levels two to five of the spirit. That is to say, as a nursery world, a level three world is intended to hold mainly level one spirit, a level four will hold mainly level two, a level five will hold mainly level three and so on. Note I say "mainly". In all cases, a scattering of other levels will incarnate there for the challenge of being either more or less spiritually developed than the populace, but of course, the challenge of this differs enormously from the challenge presented by this on Earth.

The lessons learned in these worlds differ as they do through the levels of spirit, and the form of the incarnated spirit also differs, so that in the most evolved worlds you find the gaseous form. You may see from this, that the level of a planet has a direct correlation to the advancement of its race, but this can only be the case with inhabited planets. Uninhabited planets still go through exactly the same stages of progression, but the speed of this is not related to anything but the planets own developing energies.

Planets exist for billions of our years before they are occupied by spirit in any form. The planet is always established over a lengthy time before it is decided what form the inhabiting life will take. All planets that hold life have taken their turn as a nursery world at some time, but all planets that exist and do not hold life, will not necessarily do so. Some that exist but do not hold life may do so, however, in the time to come.

The cycle of a planet is different for each. It is one of the things that is established during the "setting up" of a planet, both those that hold life and those that do not. A planet has a similar ladder of levels to complete, but the difference is that when it evolves to the highest level, it just remains there, unlike spirit that eventually returns to the Collective. A planet will just "be", continue to exist at its highest evolved level. Those that hold life will at that time be home mainly, even exclusively, to higher evolved spirit. The ladder of progression for a planet as noted, spans seven stages, but levels within the stages are not defined.

What makes the present time so interesting spiritually, is that planet Earth is due to go up a level, to move from a stage three world to a stage four world. The intended year for this to happen is 2012. The universe evolves according to a prearranged scheme. Cosmic alignments change, the forces binding the universe alter in strength and composition. Planet Earth, like all other planets, is linked with the rest of the celestial bodies by energy lines invisible to our human eye. The ancient Mayans had great astronomical skill. They saw a cataclysmic change on 21 December 2012 and interpreted it as the end of the planet. Thankfully for us, that was an error. What they saw was alignments giving rise to Earth changing level.

THE PLANETARY PLAN

Just as an individual must have a specific plan in place before incarnation, so a plan is written for the planet. "Earth has a progression plan" is an extraordinary statement to make. The scientists judge a hypothesis by the quality of the evidence, so what is mine? I cannot provide proof but circumstantial evidence, which includes the extinction of dinosaurs, the writings of Nostradamus, the existence of ancient civilisations such as

13

Ancient Egypt out of sync with the general level of development, some incredibly unlikely victors in certain battles and some parallels in the history of certain states. I will look at these in turn.

How the natural disaster, some sixty million years ago that led to the extinction of dinosaurs and most other life-forms happened, has long been a subject of scientific debate. Why it did, is that spiritually, this was an intended event so that new evolutionary paths for species could occur. Earth was designed to be the next nursery world for spirit of the level that now takes human form here. All life forms have a spiritual element and incarnate by the design of the Collective (my preferred term for God), but everything that occurs on Earth is either directly or indirectly for the benefit of the spirit that can take human form.

Dinosaurs had outlived their usefulness in a manner of speaking; their evolution was not going to progress much further than it had, and because man would not be able to co-exist alongside these creatures, they were allowed to become extinct, indeed, it was required that they did. This is my first piece of circumstantial evidence of a plan at work; the reason for the apparent planetary disaster is that it allowed man eventually to evolve.

My second piece of supporting evidence is very direct. I have related in previous books that the Collective is the grand architect of all, all planets, all species and all events. I have also described the Universal Spirit Council, which is the "working body" of the Collective, implementing the design. Nostradamus was a serving member of Council prior to and after his incarnation, in which he wrote a detailed prediction of events for five hundred years (five hundred to 1999), albeit in coded form. The task of Council is to produce plans to the Collective's grand design and see that they are implemented and distributed. A good comparison here would be a picture already drawn in charcoal, requiring others to fill in the colours or detail.

Plans are made for a cycle at a time, a cycle being two thousand years. The Collective knows all for infinity, but the plans to fit the design are arranged for a cycle ahead, or at least, that is on Earth.

On other less volatile worlds, they may be arranged for infinitely longer periods. On Earth, because freewill choice to make incorrect decisions is exercised more frequently, or at least let us say the less advanced route is chosen, it is difficult to go more than one cycle ahead. The plan is in place to the end of our current two thousand year cycle, on until 3999. The plan for the two thousand years following that is currently being designed and will be in place well before the current cycle is complete.

To return to Nostradamus, he was a high level five spirit trying to complete an incarnation with a plan to teach and bring enlightenment to his time. At the time he lived, he had great difficulties with his contemporaries, those of resistance, dogma, and jealousy, fear of being left out and of being usurped. The best he could achieve was to leave his predictions in coded form, some of which no longer exist today, in the hope that those on the spiritual path would find, read and understand his message.

Those familiar with the predictions of Nostradamus will know that grim news features prominently, wars, pestilence and so on. I have written previously to explain the spiritual purpose and reasoning behind manmade and natural disasters. It is of little comfort to know perhaps, but it is the case, that illness, war and many of the things that are tools on nursery worlds and those of lesser development, do not feature at all in higher evolved worlds.

The world plan is written to be compatible with the planet's own evolving energies and the energy influences upon it from other parts of the cosmos. Certain world events are included in the script appropriate for the stage of development of the highest life-form, homo sapiens in our case. Variety and contrast are features of individual spirit journeys, and a planetary plan will be written similarly. Extremes will be created to both give experience of such situations for younger spirit, and to provide challenge and opposition for older spirit, to change the situation to a more balanced one. Just as we have a "library" of plans to look at for inspiration and ideas in planning our individual lives, so spirit Council can look at previous plans for beginner worlds and draw upon them.

MEMORY OF LIFE ELSEWHERE

I digress to say we all have a planet of origin or "home" planet, that is the first planet we incarnate upon. It follows that for all older spirit currently on Earth, this is not their home planet, because it has held the highest variety of spirit so briefly. This may help explain why some people feel they do not belong here, why they cannot understand the behaviour of other people. We have in our regression with mediumship workshops occasionally been given the name of another planet on which a person had a past life. Some are not in our galaxy, some have a name that cannot be translated, as communication there is by vibration alone.

Although the guide tightly controls memories of non-Earth lives, we do have from our regression workshops and from mediumship, some evidence of those lives. We lose memories of past lives temporarily on incarnation on Earth, but some can be recalled in meditation or regression, some even spontaneously. Most of these memories feature lives on Earth or worlds with a similar life-form to that of Earth, but spirit in fact, does not incarnate into a life-form in some places. We have had an enquirer for mediumship called Rob who had an affinity with cold and having the feeling of being a swirl of evolving gas. We confirmed this was an extraterrestrial life memory. He had incarnated on a planet where the life-form no longer needs the solidity of a physical form in order to achieve the experiences they are incarnating to achieve. On this world the beings exist in the form of a vapour; the climate is extremely cold, frost and ice cover the entire world. It would not support life in the form we are familiar with, hence the inhabitants having evolved to the point of existing as vapour. The planet was not always this way, and the life-forms were not always this evolved, but it has been this way for longer than Earth has supported life as we know it.

All communication in that world is by thought transference, and as the incarnated souls of the world know the spiritual truths, they do not suffer the amnesia on incarnation that we all suffer on Earth. On the planet I speak of, all incarnated beings are level three or above. No one below a level three is evolved enough to be allowed to incarnate without amnesia and to practice the thought transference required to exist in that world. In the form they inhabit on that world, there is no physical interference in the spiritual development. They incarnate purely for the purpose of advancing their spiritual levels.

Sometimes we do not have a conscious memory, but a feeling we cannot explain. In my own case, I have an attraction to Scotland. The scenery there has a relaxing influence, almost a sense of "home". The first thought would possibly be that I had a past incarnation there, but on enquiry of spirit, this feeling is because I had a past incarnation in a world where the landscape is strikingly similar to the scenery in Scotland. In that world the inhabiting species had no need for a physical form. All was in essence and power of thought.

Among our enquirers for mediumship, we have met several people who felt drawn to Scotland without understanding why. It is because Scotland has a physical resemblance to a world of great spirituality. It accounts for the number of spiritual people who, on finding themselves there from other parts of our world, feel at home, feel a connection, a draw to the place. It is not Scotland exactly that draws them, but an inner recognition of this other place. Of course, it follows that those more aware will be the ones to make this recognition; it also follows that those more aware are more likely to uproot and follow their inclination to move to the place that holds this sway with them; it therefore follows that there will be a high concentration of spiritual people in Scotland.

MODERN TIMES

To continue with some further evidence of planning that underlies the whole of human history, one can look at some of the most unlikely victories in wars that have occurred. Among many such instances are some of the English victories against the French in the Middle Ages where they were far from home and greatly outnumbered, which seem incredulous. Henry V's victory at Agincourt in 1415 for example, is an instance of a dramatic victory snatched from seemingly certain defeat when he was outnumbered by five to one.

In spirit, not only is war known in advance, but also the outcome is known, and by hook or by crook, the outcome is always as intended. It may, on occasion, be seen where a particular seemingly inconsequential action has far reaching changes to the fortunes of a particular adversary. There are several instances in World War Two of Germany being helped away from a seemingly winning position; the Battle of Britain, the Battle of the Atlantic, the Battle of Stalingrad. Each time there was spirit intervention to prevent the "wrong" side winning, or rather the intended loser doing so. At Agincourt, an example of what may appear as an inevitable conclusion was suddenly reversed. As I said, the outcome is always as intended; this is a visible example of the plan at work.

Further to this, the vagaries of war, the waxing and waning of the fortunes of the participants are definitely built into the plan. The leaders have, in fact, very little sway as to the outcome. There can be, due to freewill choice of a major participant, a slight deviation in course, but it is only ever slight, as spirit will have contingencies in place to steer any such deviation quickly back on track.

We have just celebrated in England the two hundredth anniversary of Nelson's victory at the battle of Trafalgar. It was an overwhelming one, but written into the world plan as such. England was destined to be a global power and trading nation and this victory paved the way for it. All the commanders at Trafalgar, as at all battles, would have had spirit guides helping the intended result come about. Nelson's destiny was to be the heroic role model and his death went according to plan also. As his biographers pointed out, he seemed aware of it on some level, ignoring advice that day to be inconspicuous on the deck of the *"HMS Victory"*.

Another clue to a plan at work lies in two countries that have followed a similar blueprint for their development. A recent example of this is England and North America. Both have experienced civil war and the breaking away from an external power; both have, for a period, been the powerhouses of inventions in the world and both have also been the dominant power in the world. England, of course, broke away from Rome under Henry VIII; the American War of Independence was 1776. The English Civil War was 1642, the American 1862. England in the late eighteenth and early nineteenth centuries was the "workshop of the world". America took over that mantle following World War Two. England, of course, was the founder of a world Empire between 1815 and 1918. The USA has been "global policeman" since 1945. There have been other historical examples too, where two areas of the planet are intended to be similar in their culture and eventual outcome, and the same development plan has been used for both.

Looking back, one can see the Enlightenment movement in Europe had its place in the grand scheme of things. Something was needed to displace religion as the dominant ideology in the West, and to foster technological development. The flowering of intellectual thought, which rejected all metaphysics that constituted the movement, was the world plan in operation. Few academic works will discuss it in quite these terms, demonstrating how successful the new ideology has become! The challenge now is for scientists to discard their blinkered approach of insisting on observable evidence, and for them to discover spiritual concepts.

OUTSIDE HELP

There is only one nursery world at any one time. There are others at differing levels, from "just above nursery world" to "highest level". Earth has been visited from time to time by the life-forms from other planets. Some stayed for a period of time, and brought their knowledge, evidence of which is visible from their architecture. Ancient Egypt is one example of this, as I discussed in my second book, an example of a visiting civilisation, which came to foster Earth's development but eventually gave up the attempt.

One unsolved mystery for the scientists is how the pyramids came to be constructed, and I offer the answer as part of the evidence for knowledge imported from elsewhere. Sound and the use of dimension were the tools used. There are children today of advanced spirituality who have been born with an inner knowledge of their use, which is to be rediscovered in their later life. Our history books picture hundreds of slaves moving tons of stone blocks to amazing heights, stone blocks that in some cases were quarried at great distance from the point of their actual use.

The truth is that men were used in their hundreds, but for other tasks. The actual placing of the blocks was not in any of the ways scientists have tried to devise. Indeed, recent experiments carried out are leading toward the inescapable belief that it could not have been done. Given the level of technology supposedly available to the populace, the pyramids could not have been built! When it is successfully confirmed that construction could not be achieved by any method within the capabilities of the time, then the scientists will be obliged to look for other explanations. Those who were considered too offbeat in their thinking will come to be viewed in a different light and their deductions will be reinvestigated and re-examined.

THE CURRENT SITUATION

To return now to my discussion of the evolution of the planet, where are we now and where are we going? Earth is currently at level one or stage three, and it is planned it will elevate to level two or stage four in the current cycle. (More of this I discuss in the next chapter). The invention of writing or an equivalent means of recording data signifies an important step in nursery world evolution. It is an achievement needed before progression from level one to level two. (Level one is of course stage three of the seven spoken of earlier).

To move on from level one, it is necessary for the population to raise its vibration, which is achieved by an increase in awareness of spirit. There is a connection between the spiritual level of a planet and its human or human-equivalent population in that the vibrations of both are interconnected. The two must be raised simultaneously when it happens.

The general state that a planet needs to achieve in order to begin the elevation now required is for its populace to be one, to truly be brethren. While our planet has divisions of country, race, religion and so on, this cannot be. In higher evolved worlds, one is a child of the planet (or even the universe, or even not of that restriction). One accepts the beliefs of the planet, not of this or that country, or this or that religion. In addition, for a planet to be able to advance, it requires the populace to harmonise with the planet, rather than to rape it.

Looking back at world history, one can see choices have been missed and are still being missed to begin the elevation of Earth. Both the Roman and the British empires, for example, had the potential to unite countries. They were attempts to do this by control, the intention being that it would be observed that this was not the way, and each as we know, turned out to be empires built on sand.

More obvious historical missed chances were those following the two World Wars. The League of Nations and the United Nations both have not met the expectations of the founders in being the vehicle to end war. In current times, the Bush Administration's rejection of the Kyoto treaty on global warming, the attempt to change energy policy in favour of the planet was a missed opportunity. However, further opportunities will present themselves.

There are examples of harmonising with the planet that can be brought to mind. Sadly these have been only with isolated groups or there has been a slide backwards as soon as they depart. These examples are the spiritual peoples throughout history, the North American Indians, the Aborigines, the Druids and Pagans and others; people who respected the earth and sought to nourish it, so that in turn, it continues to nurture them. In falling back, the plan was still followed. These cultures will serve as comparison in future when man does seek the better way.

How does one explain the paradox then, that if Earth needs to raise its vibration, why have spiritual peoples been so devastated by Europeans; the Incas, Indians and Aborigines for example? The overall plan does not just call for greater challenges to such people, but the recognition by the destroyers of the "rightness" of these peoples. If they had not existed to be so devastated, there

21

would be nothing for the white man to use as comparison to his own ways. From a few people realising that these peoples were, in fact, the more spiritually evolved than the so-called civilized white man who acted in a most barbaric fashion in his decimation of these peoples, so others are realising who possessed the far greater spirituality.

Now it is beginning to be understood that living in houses with solid walls of brick or stone and roofs of slate and tile, rather than in mud huts or collapsible tents, does not signify man's development, except in a material sense. These peoples, though backward in material terms, were in fact the enlightened ones. Had they not existed to be so decimated, they would not be in man's history to be reflected on. The comparison could not be made. Those that begin to have this same realisation at this time could not have made it had this not been the case.

Their purpose therefore, was not only to provide those spirits with the challenges and life plans they were provided with, but that their decimation would play its part in the raising of the universal consciousness of the planet. The means of progression of a planet is for its peoples to raise the vibration by their own growth and in the plan for Earth, these and other peoples played their part in setting the comparison with the modern way of life, so we may come to realise what has been lost.

RELIGION

Before concluding this chapter, I should discuss "spirituality" and "religion", as in the mind of many these are automatically associated concepts. In fact, spirituality has no connection with religion whatsoever, not even as cousins, let alone siblings. One could list a whole catalogue of historical events that show religion has no link to spirituality.

Where was the spiritual understanding of the Spanish Inquisition, or the Bloody Terror of the reign of Mary Tudor? Where is the spiritual understanding of our religious wars in the Middle East or even on our own doorstep in Ireland? Where is the spiritual understanding of our local "Christian" communities, who judge,

who look down on others? Where is the spiritual understanding of
our churchmen who for centuries have ruled by fear and dogma,
suppressing anything that may weaken their hold on the
populace?

Religion has been used by a minority as a vehicle for power and
control over the majority. True spirituality is recognition of the
equality of each individual person, who must be allowed freewill
choice to discover for himself what is correct and what is not. Did
not ancient cultures have a strong religious element to them?

Modern man has put a religious interpretation on the use of the
temples of Ancient Egypt, but this is in fact a distortion. The
pyramids were buildings for communication and the Pharaohs
were accorded the honour of being buried in them. On departure
from this world, much of the content of the pyramids was
removed, so that they now appear to be only burial chambers.

The temples were also not what they appear. Temples to Isis, Ra
and so on, were in fact places of learning, places for spiritual
progression, not temples in the accepted sense. Those chosen for
what I have previously termed as the priesthood were, in fact,
those that were granted the benefit of this spiritual progression;
their being chosen was based entirely upon their existing degree of
spirituality. The tuition received in the varying temples dealt
with different aspects of the spiritual knowledge or "unconditional
love". Thus in the temple of Isis would be learned the female
aspect of mother love among other things. Through time, this has
been interpreted as Isis being considered the mother goddess. So
it was with all the "Gods". Gods is a term that has come about by
interpretation. What would be a better description, might be
teachers, disciplines, sages, or Masters. They delivered the
teachings on the differing aspects of unconditional love, which the
visitors sought to pass on to their earthly counterparts through
admission to the ranks of a particular "temple". The temple
should, in fact, be called a university. Those who were allowed to
have brief "lessons" by visiting on occasion were privileged, those
who were allowed to enrol for the whole course were the more so.

Those who followed the visitors by birth gradually misconstrued the concepts, and present day archaeologists have completed the misconception. This is not difficult to understand, when one realises that it is only now, spiritual information is coming to the fore. In a world where until now religion was usually the foremost answer to everything, it is easy to see why it would be interpreted as this. A similar misunderstanding has been applied by modern man to the ancient standing stone circles in Western Europe. These were not for religious purposes, but in fact, were centres of healing.

It is a paradox that simultaneously with the decline of religion in the West and the rise of the culture of consumerism, religious extremism such as Islamic Fundamentalism has flourished in other parts of the world. If one looks at known history, one can see that religious extremism and fanaticism have been used on Earth as a regular theme. Atrocities, pain and suffering and countless misguided acts and events have been committed in the name or religion by those who had little doubt that they were acting in the interests of their God, or who just seized the opportunity of the moment for self advancement through it!

In the present time, religious zeal is used in the plan in conjunction with the decline in religious fervour by countries that themselves experienced religious fanaticism many years ago. It can now be seen by Western countries, how unnecessary such extremism is and will result in a raised awareness and an increase in the search for meaning. This leads me to offer a summary from the spiritual perspective of what each planet must experience in making the transition from nursery world to the next level:

By the time the planet is no longer deemed a nursery world the race has evolved through being a race of beginners, open to spirit even in their raw state, because they are not sufficiently evolved to question, through being a race mixed in their ability, civilised to the point of losing their spirituality but still having an element that retain it, through being completely non-spiritual and back to the reawakening of their spirituality.

To further explain, the inhabitants are given spiritual knowledge in the first instance, then some development takes place where, for some, spirituality is lost, then a period of complete non-spirituality, and then going full circle, back to the knowledge; going backwards in order to go forward. Of course, I am speaking of knowledge of spirit here, recognition that we are spiritual beings in a human form and so on, nothing to do with religion. This is why we live in interesting times and now is a preferred time to incarnate here. It is a huge challenge for the planet's population to make the necessary changes in perception and awareness. I discuss more of this cycle of losing spirituality to the point of almost complete disaster, before it is regained once more in the next chapter, when I quote verbatim channelled teachings.

CHAPTER TWO

LIFE ELSEWHERE

*"What a piece of work is a man! How noble in reason! how
infinite in faculty! in form, in moving, how express and
admirable! in action how like an angel! in apprehension how
like a god! the beauty of the world! the paragon of animals!
And yet, to me, what is this quintessence of dust? man
delights not me;"*

Shakespeare described man wonderfully in *"Hamlet"* and his
genius is worth a reminder. His conclusion hints at knowledge of
life elsewhere. We have, of course, nothing to compare ourselves
with as a species, so I asked our guide if man is unique in the form
that we are in the universe. I have previously said visitors to
Earth in the case of Ancient Egyptians were human-like, and I
have learned of "inspectors" from another world who arrived for a
short visit and were also human-like in outward appearance.
Here is the reply received from spirit:

*"Life in some other worlds is humanoid in appearance. There are
differences in internal function, differences in emotional make up,
but for some life-forms, the surface appearance is not unlike that of
humans. There are others of course which bear no resemblance,
think of the gaseous incarnation of your friend Rob. There is more
than one world where this is the norm. So, while each race is
unique in form, there are striking similarities in physical
appearance between some. What is different in man, is his
emotional and mental make-up. This is unique to the human
species.*

*Again, the emotional and mental make up of each race is unique to
itself, but some bear strong resemblances to each other. Man is
alone in his stubborn refusal to lift himself to the higher
consciousness needed to progress spiritually. Most races, even
though they undergo their period as nursery school, are eager to
leave that stage, to move on so that they may attract higher level*

26

spirit and enjoy a more harmonious environment. They may not consciously be aware that this is the reason they wish to evolve until they have done so, but have the intelligence to understand that they need to progress emotionally and spiritually and not just technically.

Man has a greater level of certain emotions and tendencies in his genetic make up than any other race before. He has a greater need to possess and control, a greater greed, a greater disregard for life, a greater self-centredness and a greater cruelty than any race previously. This is not an accident; this was known when the "species" was designed. The intention was to create a race that could provide more challenges in a life than had been available previously and so aid spiritual progression in this way. It has, however, contributed to man being slow to take the step of spiritual progression that is now required, so that earth may become a planet of higher spiritual consciousness and another nursery planet may begin its cycle.

As Earth is little behind in this regard, we are giving it assistance to take the step by arranging for more high level spirit to incarnate there currently and in the future. As I said yesterday, the next one hundred years will see a great change in the spiritual make up of man. Unfortunately, as I also said, there will be an increase in disasters before this fully happens. To clarify, this refers to an increase in both natural and manmade disaster. I think the news you have witnessed today will prove this point! Think, children being born now will be twenty-five to thirty of your years at the very least, before they can be in the positions that they are incarnating to take."

Some words of explanation for certain references:

- ❖ "Friend Rob" is the one referred to previously, who remembers being a swirling gas.
- ❖ "We are giving assistance" refers to members of Spirit Council, responsible for overseeing the planet.
- ❖ "News witnessed today" refers to the World Trade Centre attack in New York on 11 September 2001, the day we received this answer. No coincidence perhaps that we

were "on line" that day!

I now wish to introduce the topic and relevance of natural earth energies (ley lines, ley rivers) to an understanding of the present state of the world. To explain these, they are a web of lines and rivers across the surface of the whole planet. They were established by the Creator or Source when the planet was first formed. Their purpose is to carry the vital life-force or energy necessary for life to exist. This energy arrives on the planet from the stars. Our Sun is a principal source. Modern science has yet to recognise this energy which I term "universal energy," as it is found everywhere in the universe. It is this energy that all spiritual healers use in their work. This energy is needed by the soul on a daily basis, just as the body needs food and oxygen. The energy also makes the planet a living, evolving thing.

When damaged, the planet suffers ills, as will humans and mammals who come into contact with such energy. Sensitivity to the energies varies between people, older spirit are the more sensitive generally. However, whether sensitive or not, everyone will be affected by the condition of the energies, whether healthy and balanced or unhealthy and soured. When balanced, a sense of well-being, inner peace and love is engendered. When unbalanced, feelings of irritability, short-temper and intolerance often arise. Unbalanced energies can give rise to certain health problems. These have been labelled "sick building syndrome" and "geopathic stress". On a planetary level, earthquakes, drought, floods, and so on occur because of an energy imbalance, or if not will create one as a consequence in the vicinity, which will then increase the likelihood of a future natural disaster.

I will discuss the technicalities of earth energies in a future book, but first I wish to show their importance to the health of all life. I asked the question, *"What are the consequences of an unhealthy planet for mankind and of soured ley lines for individuals and communities please?"*

Our guide replied, *"To answer this, it would be better to ask what the consequences of a healthy planet without soured ley lines would be. You are already living with the results of the above scenario.*

If the energy carried by the ley and the energy rivers were flowing as it should be, your planet would enjoy a greater peace and harmony, a greater love by its populace of its fellow man, fewer wars, atrocities and acts of needless violence, less famine, drought and natural disaster. This is the simple answer, but as usual, the full explanation is more complex.

Let us follow through the chain of events on your planet. From its very creation, the planet has had ley lines and energy-rivers. Before there was any life of any description, flora or fauna, the lines and rivers existed as they do on all planets. It was decided that Earth should become the next nursery planet and so life was introduced. Species were gradually added, but did no harm to the infrastructure of the planet's energy supply. Then, as was the purpose of the whole exercise, man incarnated on Earth. In the beginning, he did not affect the energy of the planet.

In these early times, there were those incarnating who brought with them the knowledge to harness the world's energy, to use it for their good and the good of their world. In other areas, "visitors" taught the knowledge to man. Still the energy of the planet was not affected.

Man was a being of raw emotion, providing for incarnating spirit the range of experiences always provided by all new-life forms on nursery planets but to an even greater degree than previously. Still however, he did not affect the energy of the planet. Natural disasters occurred, man inflicted cruelty on man, wars were fought, but all of these were as they were meant to be; designed to provide these experiences not available in more mature worlds, and still the energy of the planet was not affected.

Then as man became more "civilised", he began to interfere with the natural order of things. This was caused by his inventions, his technology, his science, and his very civilisation! The knowledge was gradually forgotten as none were allowed to incarnate with it from this time, and the visitors no longer taught it. As with all species, man had reached the point where possession of the knowledge would be dangerous for his world. It would be like giving a sub-machine gun to a child.

It was always known, of course, that this interference with the planet's energies would occur, that the planet's energy would be damaged. That as a result of the damage, more natural disaster would occur, more war, more atrocity, and so on through the list. This is the pattern that has always occurred on developing planets. However, on most others, the nature of the intelligent species is such that it quickly spots the problem and moves onward in its development. Moves onward by moving backwards, backwards to its true spiritual nature.

The damage done to the energies on these planets is only temporary, a result of adolescence, like a rash of spots on a developing teenager. A blemish on perfection caused by changing body chemistry, but quickly outgrown. So it was with the damage to the energies of these planets. A manifestation of the changing circumstances, but quickly outgrown. These planets then returned to their natural harmony. Their inhabitants moved on to become races of spiritually advanced beings. All of the negative emotions experienced on Earth ceased to exist in these worlds. You realise, in this we are covering a period of millions and millions of your years and that this did not happened on all life-supporting planets at the same time. As each reached a certain point in the evolution of its species, (actually, the point is when the species recognise and return to the spiritual way) the next nursery planet begins its life. This is the way it has always been.

Other races may not have been created to be genetically as extreme with their negative emotion and experiences in the first instance as is man, may not have indulged in war to the same degree, but all have had the progression of moving through negative situations of some sort, to become the beings they now are.

Then we have man!

Your race has followed the blue print of development. It was always known that in man we had created a being that would provide genetically for a greater range of experience for incarnating spirit; a being that would almost gladly embrace the negative and destructive emotions of a young and developing race; a being that would appear to enjoy the very negative state that most strive to leave behind as quickly as possible. As you know, all is planned in spirit but genetic tendencies do provide for the experiences chosen by incarnating spirit. Also, as the majority on any nursery planet are level one, there is more failure to achieve life-plan than on other worlds where the level is generally higher. Failure to achieve life-plan happens at all levels, but it is true to say the percentage is higher among level ones. But as all is planned in spirit, it is no surprise to us that the world is the way it is, but now it is time for it to move on.

As you know, you are experiencing a period of catch up. This is not only a catching up in the area of your technologies, but in the area of your understanding and acceptance of man's true spiritual identity and nature. More and more respected researchers are working in the field of what they loosely term the paranormal, and as you know, more and more interest is being generated in the field of spiritually related studies, alternative therapies, and the like. Matters of this kind have become vogue. Do you think this is coincidence? Surely not; by now you know that no such thing exists! It is time for the world to move on and in order to achieve this, more high level spirit than normal will incarnate in your world over the next one hundred years to make sure that man meets the challenge. You already know about the children being born with knowingness, the children with the special gifts. Also incarnating are spirits with life-plans which will bring them into positions where they can influence the growth of man's spiritual consciousness, influence the way man views his world. Look about you, it is already happening, but very slowly. It will accelerate in the years to come.

The next step for your race and by association, for your planet is for man to stop destroying it, stop wounding it and draining it of its lifeblood. This will be a major accomplishment and you will note that work is afoot at the moment in this regard. America is proving, or I should say the powers in America are proving stubborn, but it is intended that this will change very soon. Globally, this has become an issue occupying the minds and energies of those in the public eye, so it will become vogue to work *in this way, and yes, gradually man will stop raping the planet.*

The next major achievement will be for there to be general recognition and acceptance of the method of healing the damage already done. This is were the work of the community in Lincolnshire and many others of a similar design operating in their own designated ways will come to the fore. They will already be carrying out this work and when the rest of the world suddenly discovers this "new miracle", these groups will be ready to lead for others to follow. They are being created now for when the world is ready. This will happen, it is in the plan!

Once man has reached this stage, he will be ready to return to his true spiritual nature, to become a higher evolved race, and another nursery planet will begin its life.

To return to your question, there are no consequences from an unhealthy planet for mankind, other than more of what he is currently experiencing. More of the same, and as the damage to the planet worsens, more of it happening at once. More wars occurring around the globe, more natural disaster and so on. Nothing new, just an increase in the incidents which are already part and parcel of your lives, but which need to stop.

They will stop, it is not in the plan for the world to end, there may be some major disasters to come (you realise I cannot tell you of these), which will aid man's recognition of the error of his ways in regard to his treatment of his world, but the planet will endure, life will endure."

I offer some footnotes of explanation:

> "We had created" is a reference to the Spirit Council I described in my second book.
> These "Children with the special gifts" are children described and written about as "Indigo", based on the colour of their aura. They are older spirits, choosing to incarnate with a certain mental condition, often labelled "attention disorder" or ""autistic" but not accurately so.
> "Community in Lincolnshire" – the work involved there is a

separate topic. In brief, it is a very small group dedicated to the repair of the earth energy system, and able to teach others how to do similar work elsewhere.

Clearly this is a truly amazing piece of over-arching analysis of the human condition, which is why I have quoted it verbatim. It should be e-mailed to all those politicians who have influence on the world stage! Unfortunately, they would not gladly receive it, I am sure, being not of the correct spiritual awareness to believe it and accept it and it is not in their life-plans that they do so. Hopefully those destined for future positions of influence will see it and be able to act on it, or at least have the inner knowledge of it or have been able to acquire it by some other means than this book.

As I have to remind myself, the value lies in discovery of the spiritual truths for oneself. To be told them or to accept them because they have become fashionable does not count as personal growth and therefore achievement. The great paradox is everyone knows the spiritual truths in their spirit state. The challenge is to rediscover them in the incarnated state. This is a challenge that is not for everyone; it belongs to those nearing the end of the long syllabus of experiences.

To return to the philosophy, I needed clarification how to reconcile life-plans with the fact the planet is damaged. The spiritual reasoning is as follows, said our guide:

"Every disaster that happens on your planet (on any planet) is known in advance. Manmade ones are of course, the result of life-plans of those incarnating and natural ones can be either the result of man's actions or caused by nature itself.

Let us first take the case of a natural disaster caused by natural circumstances. This is perhaps the easiest for you to comprehend. Spirit, because of its communion with the essence of your planet, knows all that is to happen to it through its weather, its changing formations, its shifts and its changes. We know every storm, every earthquake, every famine, every drought, every volcanic eruption, every tornado, everything! We actually "arrange" to a degree, that these things will occur. A little like a director choosing the props for the play. I say arrange to a degree, because it is not quite as simplistic as this and involves two-way interaction between spirit and the planet. This is complex subject. For now, just trust me to say that we know all of this because we "sort of" arrange it.

We knew the damage man would do to the planet and the worsening of the natural disasters as a result. We knew this from the outset and the plans were made to fit to this pattern.

Now, manmade disasters. Let us take war, as this is the one that occupies your curiosity most. As you quoted to my sister today, things can fail to happen that are planned, but nothing can happen that is not planned. Keep this in mind while we discuss this.

As war depends on the actions of incarnated beings, these beings of course, incarnate with these actions in their life-plan. Because of free will choice, they may be unable to carry out their plan and the war may not take place. This means that all those destined to have the variety of experiences this could have created will fail to achieve their life-plan in that incarnation. Many thousands of unachieved plans, but in the overall scheme of things, not many really. To fully understand that, you would need to see this on a universal scale or even greater, rather than on an earthly scale. Not all of those who take part in a war are necessarily to have the major plot of their lives fulfilled by the war. Their involvement in the war may be by way of a minor plot. Their experience as parents, as spouses or some other, may be their main plot. Therefore, even if the war were not to take place, it would not necessarily mean their life had failed and they may not be forced to repeat.

Having said this, those that incarnate with the plan to provide the necessary actions to cause war, seldom fail to achieve their plan. Think of how many chances you both have had to achieve parts of your plan, three times in the case of our sister's accident. You can be assured then, that EVERY assistance is given to one who's plan has a bearing on so many others, so that it may be achieved!!

To put this further into perspective, in the case of war, only twice in the entire history of your planet, even the history you are unaware of, has there been a case of a planned war not occurring.

So, a war that is planned may not occur (although this is extremely rare), but one that does occur is definitely planned. Having planned it, then the fact that it is to occur is freely known to spirit thirds so that life-plans may be scripted to use the unique scenarios it can offer. Even those who are to be responsible for it are cast when the time is right, although the fact that the time would be right will have been known in spirit for all time.

When you asked if the future is known before it happens, I told you that major events such as world wars are scheduled, but not the exact times and dates or even the exact players, just that they will happen and need to be scripted when the time is right.

This is it exactly. Spirit knows for all time, all of these events that may take place on your world. When it is time, the players are arranged. The player may miss his cue, and even after several prompts, may still not complete his part and then there may not be a war, but if there is, it has been known for all time that it would occur.

I used war as the example, but the same is true of all manmade incidents.

With regard to damage to the planet, as I said earlier, we knew it would happen, in fact, planned that it would and the range of life experiences it has afforded has been available because of it. Now, it is time for it to stop and as we knew he would, man is resisting the changes that he needs to make. Plans are in the pipeline to deal with this, plans that have again been known for all time.

It seemed to me the simple solution is level fives in government. Our guide confirmed this and said,

"Of course, and now that it is time for change, those that are to take these roles are incarnating to do so. I told you this last night when I said "more high level spirit than normal will incarnate in your world over the next one hundred years to make sure that man meets the challenge". They are incarnating now and will take their

place to assist the world to change, but they need to grow up first! During this time, things will get worse to get better. Again, this was the plan, those incarnating now are doing so to be in the right place at the right time years hence. We do not leave things to the last minute! This is all as expected. The period of catch up for technology is obvious, what is not so obvious is the period of catch up taking place for mankind's future spiritual growth, but it is taking place!

When you have level fives in leadership roles, they will indeed be able to make the changes that lead the race into a communion with their planet, and so precipitate the change to the race necessary for it to become a higher evolved spiritual race. This will stop any more damage to the planet in time.

This will take time however, and although it will stop any further damage, it is still necessary to repair the damage already done. This is the reason for the need for groups such as the community in Lincolnshire and all the others globally preparing for this task in their differing ways.

So, the damage to the planet will be stopped by those in positions of power, but the people will need education in the spiritual way, will require teaching what to put in place of what is familiar to them, and they will look around for examples to follow as they always do. They will find groups such as the one in Lincolnshire and adopt the teachings and examples they can offer. So the reason for these groups is two-fold, repair of existing damage and education into the new "old" way."

The message quoted at the beginning of this chapter included the statement *"Man is alone in his stubborn refusal to lift himself to the higher consciousness needed to progress spiritually"*. Misguidedly, I took some exception to this remark. Perhaps this was because I personally have spent much time and effort in raising my own awareness. At the risk of repetition, therefore, I should like to expand on the spiritual thinking behind that statement for the benefit of any reader who may have felt similarly. The elaboration received is as follows:

All is planned, all is arranged; my phrase about stitching your thread on a tapestry already outlined is most apt in describing the writing of a life-plan. Man has not the power to choose his future, so he cannot really be held accountable for the war and natural disasters and so on. To recap and see if this helps our clarity on this, one can list the following:

1   Earth is a nursery world.
2   Because Earth is a nursery world, the baser emotions, the negative experiences are experienced and played out here more than elsewhere.
3   It is now time for Earth to move on, in this planetary cycle anyway.
4   There has been a period of catch-up so that Earth may be ready to move on.
5   The catch-up was necessary, as various choices were not taken at the time when they were first introduced, and so they have needed to be accelerated by the incarnation of some higher level spirit with the knowledge to bring them to fruition.
6   In this way, the future is known, but a bit of rescripting may be required to make sure it meets certain time boundaries such as the end of a cycle.
7   It has taken Earth longer than most worlds to reach the point of "graduation".
8   It was planned by spirit that it would take Earth longer than others had taken.
9   It was planned in spirit that man would take longer to recognise his spirituality than on other worlds.
10   Man should by now be "raising his vibration" and using war on the next level, as a means of recognition of spirituality.
11   This will happen as all is known and planned, but we may need a bit of rescripting to catch up, just as with technology.

When a planet has experienced war for all the negative experiences and souls have gained the spiritual enlightenment from that, the natural progression in other worlds is to become sickened by it, to see the futility of it, to realise the spiritual truth, that we are all part of the whole, and that to declare war on others is to damage ourselves. War then presents what our guide referred to as the next level of development, the bonding together of the majority in an outcry against this futile way of settling difference, a move towards addressing the cause rather than reacting against the symptoms. A universal coming together of a planet as one race, all thinking and acting in unison, but by design, not because of the power of a few.

"This is what we would hope will come from the current conflict, not immediately, but from the conflict I spoke of which will be born out of this present one concerning Bin Laden.

Man does need to catch up in this regard, but there are those who are incarnated and incarnating in order to bring this about. Of course, by this I refer to those who are to be the catalyst for it, the warmongers, as well as those destined to be the peacemakers.

Again then, Earth has needed and does need war, but should be having the elevated response to it by now. It was planned that this would take longer that in other worlds, but now choices have been missed and are being missed to begin this elevation. We need to script in and are scripting in "catch up" to make sure it takes place as planned.

We knew there would be resistance to it, and knew that we would need to intervene in both this and the technological progression. We did not plan that wrong choices would be made, but in so many cases, contingency plans were and are in place to bring the necessary ones to the crossroads a second and third time. If they still take the wrong path, then others are incarnating to follow in their stead. Earth will arrive, but this is why we allow the five hundred year leeway spoken of above.

It is hard for you to see the way of this whilst incarnated, all of this is natural in spirit, but is hard to grasp in an Earthly existence.

To say that man needs to "raise his vibration" is not a criticism as you have perceived it, more a statement. He does need to do this. We knew it would be resisted, we knew it would take second and third attempts, which is why they were planned into the necessary lives. We knew even then, some would fail and so others were arranged to follow. All of this, to arrive at the point where man raises his vibration, and moves towards the elevation of the planet. It may take 500 years of so, to achieve this, but it will be achieved, it is planned that way!

The reference to man's stubborn refusal to raise his vibration, was not really incorrect either. Those that incarnate on Earth with a part to play in this next important step have to struggle against the attitudes, beliefs and negativity that they find here, if they are to complete their plan. It is easier to take the wrong path, make the wrong decisions, because of the influence of others. Of course, this is the very thing that makes incarnation on Earth such a challenge, and so the choice of high-level spirit. Man is, by making these wrong choices, clinging to what is familiar action, rather than seeking a higher route. He will take the higher route, there is no option in that, the only question is how long it will take him, how many times we need to insert a contingency route into a plan and how many higher spirits we will need to send to lift the level to one that man will continue to support.

Some have made headway with this during your history, but either only with isolated groups or the slide back has followed as soon as they depart.

As you rightly say, man does not choose the future, that is arranged in spirit, but the prevailing attitudes on a planet can dictate timing of that future to a degree, and this is what is occurring."

A microcosm of what may be a future pattern of global events is the experiences of Sri Lanka. For twenty years the country was plagued by a civil war in which over sixty thousand died and a million become refugees, which recently came to an end at the time of writing. On 15 March 2002, a large number of people gathered for a "peace meditation". Their purpose was *"to change the collective consciousness about war and peace – to make war unthinkable and peace inevitable"*. An estimated six hundred and fifty thousand people gathered to meditate for one hour, and in doing so, radiated a powerful consciousness for the cause of peace.

The "ordinary villagers" who took part will have gained a sense of personal responsibility for the creation of peace, their spirituality strengthened by participation. The sadness is that it took such a long period of civil and ethnic war to bring this communal change in consciousness. The channelled teachings spoke of a period of catch-up in technologies and our true spiritual nature. In the next chapter I look at something of the "motor" of technological advance that has so accelerated recently.

CHAPTER THREE

THE ASCENT OF MAN

The year 2003 marked the centenary of man's first flight. What an illustration of very rapid great technological leaps, from first faltering flight of just a few yards to supersonic travel around the globe. It is a sobering thought to go back, say, six hundred years in history. We were fighting each other with bows and arrows and swords and now we have the stealth bomber, cruise missiles et al. What has happened to bring this about in that six hundred years, or more amazingly, in the last century, if one takes the history of flight time frame? A century is a mere blink of the eye of course, compared to the age of the Earth.

Have our brains suddenly changed in size? Has our intelligence rapidly multiplied? Darwin taught us evolution takes place often over a very long period of time and is due to pressure of survival. What evolutionary pressures can explain this amazing burst in the discovery and application of technology in Western man? Being able to journey through the air has no obvious survival purpose.

Can there be a religious explanation? Unlikely, as the West has seen a decline in religion and, moreover, religion is characterised by the control of thought and historically has opposed science. Is this pure chance then? Surely not, because if so, why did a human-like animal exist for tens or hundreds of thousands of years and remain a hunter-gatherer for most of that time? If due to chance, one would expect a more gradual development pattern. To get continuous throws of six on the dice of discovery cannot be due to chance.

So did it occur because of man's aggressive warlike behaviour? Was it the need for better weapons than the perceived enemy held that drove this exponential growth in applied science? Certainly wars have been a catalyst to research and invention, but man has always been warlike. It is one of his defining characteristics!

The explanation lies in none of these areas. It is explained by the fact that the whole of human existence is orchestrated and choreographed from the spirit dimension. To understand this, firstly one must appreciate that a human being is merely a container for spirit. Individual spirit incarnates here as homo sapiens to have human experiences. Not only that, but each human life is pre-planned. Beyond the planning of individual lives is the plan for the planet as a whole. The totality of human history is not a series of random or chance events, but the result of a plan, written in blocks each spanning two thousand years as discussed in the first chapter.

Each one of us has a spirit guide, whose task it is to ensure we achieve our life-plan. Guides are normally invisible to the human eye, but are being increasingly caught by digital cameras. The guides communicate many times during each day. Most of us are unaware of it, being unable to distinguish between our own thoughts and those of the guide. Guides are the mechanism by which individual life-plans, and from those, the global plan are made a reality.

The existence of the plan for the planet is the explanation for the recent burst in technological knowledge. As the planet came towards the end of one cycle in the year 1999, man was "behind schedule" in his knowledge, so spirit accelerated the introduction of scientific advances to bring him up to speed, up to the norm for a planet at the end of its nursery stage.

What may seem to be the result of a stroke of individual human genius in advancing science is, in fact, an individual spirit incorporating in his life-plan the introduction of new knowledge. Let us consider as an example the life of Isaac Newton, the founding figure of the Enlightenment movement, which ushered in the Age of Reason, to be followed by the Industrial Revolution.

Newton had great intelligence, but there is not a satisfactory nature or nurture explanation for this. His father could not sign his own name and neither parents nor grandparents had academic skill. He had a most unhappy childhood, his mother largely abandoning him when she remarried when he was aged two (his father died before he was born). Genius is a mark of talent acquired in previous lives. Newton had been a mathematician in a previous life. His intelligence was linked to his spiritual age. He was an older spirit, nearing the end of his spiritual journey. One of the tasks sometimes chosen by older spirit is the bringing of new knowledge to the place of incarnation. Newton obtained his important scientific insights through meditation. That is the classic method to obtain communication with one's guide, to clear a space in the mind to allow the guide's thoughts to come through. His genius was greatly aided by his guide giving him key insights. He was driven in his search for truth. Being driven is a big clue to being motivated by spirit and further evidence of life-plan.

PREHISTORY

Let us now go back to the beginning. First it is necessary to appreciate that there is more than one variety of spirit that all living things contain. Animals are one variety and all mammals with the exception of man constitute a category in themselves. Each spirit must stay in its category, so a mammal can only reincarnate as a mammal, therefore a cat can come back as an elephant but not as an insect, bird or fish, or as a man. Man is set apart by his intelligence and speech, and is used as a vessel for the most evolved variety of spirit that will also incarnate elsewhere using the higher evolved life form of that world.

Until about 9000BC, the variety of spirit that incarnated as Neanderthal and Homo Sapiens was animal spirit. True, that spirit had much more intelligence than some of the animal spirit we have alive today, but it was still the animal variety. That explains a number of things.

Firstly, why there was such a long period, hundreds of thousands of years, even millions according to some scientists, when an ape-like creature lived on the planet but remained a hunter-gatherer, and did not develop technology. The graph of scientific knowledge remained flat because Earth had not yet arrived at the point in its evolution which I have termed nursery world, which is the point at which it can hold the most evolved variety of spirit. A second explanation is why agriculture and settled communities developed when they did, initially in the Middle East.

There was a second time that spirit of the highest variety began to use Earth. That was around 7500BC. The life form we refer to as Neanderthal was the evolutionary end of the first life introduced. It evolved directly from Homo Erectus, who in turn, evolved from the ape family. Modern man, Homo Sapiens Sapiens, did not evolve from the Neanderthal man, but was introduced as a "new variety". There was an overlapping period following the introduction of modern man during which the Neanderthals gradually disappeared. This was because spirit preferred the new model, as once established, it was obviously evolving faster than the old. The scientists hypothesise it was because the new species was more agile and had a quicker brain pattern that drove the Neanderthal to extinction, but it was in fact because when spirit no longer requires a particular style of vessel, it will become extinct.

DARWINISM

This, of course, now gives a new perspective on Darwinism. His great discoveries recorded in *"The Origin of Species"* and *"The Descent of Man"* are correct in revealing to us biological evolution, but they are incomplete by excluding the spiritual aspects of evolution, which is firstly that all new species are designed in the spirit dimension beforehand. All life by definition must contain the universal life force and all life-forms are merely containers for use by spirit. Spirit has several varieties, the one of which we are part being the most complex variety. Secondly, each spirit surrounds itself with an energy form of DNA. It is the universal life-force passing through this energy that activates the physical DNA inside each cell that creates the life-form. In the familiar chicken and egg conundrum, it is the energy DNA of the egg that would arrive before the chicken. New species appear not spontaneously, but by spirit arriving with a new form of life blueprint. If anyone doubts that we are spirit, they might reflect on where our thoughts originate. The brain does not produce thought, it is the soul that does this, but it needs the brain to be functioning in order for it to translate this. What the many documented near death experiences show us is that consciousness can exist independently of the body. What déjà vu experiences and past life regressions show us are that spirit reincarnates.

Conventional wisdom for Darwinists is that we evolved from cavemen. In July 2002, I watched a Channel Four TV programme entitled "Sex BC". In it, a number of academics discussed erotic dolls that were around 25,000 years old. There were two main arguments. One theory was that the exaggerated breasts, stomach and hips of the dolls were Venus figurines used in worship. A problem with this hypothesis was some were found in rubbish sites, an unlikely place for religious objects. A second theory was that they were some kind of "prehistoric centrefold". The fact that the female genitals were shown, but that the dolls had no facial features, just head and hair, suggested that here was an early form of the separation of the female person from sex, thus, pornography.

Both theories show what we are prone to do, is to look at the past through modern eyes. The explanation for the dolls is that it would have been important to have children for the survival of the family group. Not all acts of intercourse would result in pregnancy, but the biological reasons for this would not be known. These dolls were therefore not erotic, but represented a wish fulfilment object that could be held, during, before or after intercourse, to ensure pregnancy. It explains the heavily pregnant form of the dolls. It was thus, a primitive type of visualisation. The dolls could be passed around or traded, hence the lack of distinctive facial features and the ones that ended up in the rubbish tip were the ones that did not work!

Does the use of dolls not indicate intelligence beyond that of an animal? The explanation is that at the present time we do not have an animal species capable of holding the highest variety of animal spirit, and so we do not recognise it. Chimpanzees are the nearest we have. The spirit of prehistoric man was still animal spirit. Just as the spirit that can be human has far more abilities than we are aware of, abilities that are at the moment used elsewhere, so the spirit that is animal has more abilities than we are used to witnessing. So man had not yet arrived for "Sex BC", but arrived about 9000BC, after the time of Atlantis.

ATLANTIS

There are many books written about Atlantis, the fabled island or land mass, inhabited by an advanced race that disappeared in a violent earthquake around 13,000 years ago. At the risk of derision, I can confirm that it was the home to a colony of what I term "visitors", from a very advanced world. They were on Earth to help over the period with the integration of the evolved variety of spirit into the form of human. When they completed their task, they left, obliterating all trace of their existence, as their city, buildings, culture and technology would have been inappropriate to be left unattended on such a backward planet and could have affected natural evolution. Their work would have included diminishing the ice caps as the planet was then in the grip of an ice age, and fine tuning the earth's energies.

OUTSIDE HELP

Earth has been helped, or at least, was intended to be helped, on a number of subsequent occasions after Atlantis. I have referred in my discussion on earth energies how visitors came to the planet to teach early man how to use the energies to heal the planet and himself, knowledge that has been lost in modern times. I attach a graph showing the extent of visitor influence in how much spiritual information there has been on Earth and how much was "local knowledge" over time since Atlantis, and where it is intended to go in the future.

All major civilisations of antiquity had some form of assistance in becoming what they were. In some cases the visitors were the guiding force, the ruling class and lived on Earth for a period of time thinking that by ruling the people they could lead them into an accelerated pattern of evolution. Not all of them were equally advanced and spiritual, but even the least advanced and spiritual were still much more so than humans. Some just sowed seeds and left them to germinate alone. Some sowed the seeds and tended them with love like a keen gardener. Some of the races concerned did not even need to have a physical presence on Earth in order to do this; they had the communication ability to achieve it without. In each case they realised that the people of Earth were not receptive, not advanced sufficiently to be able to provide a rich enough soil for the seeds to thrive in. In each case the project was abandoned, but the trying would have been in the life plans of the ones concerned from each of these races.

ANCIENT ROME EXAMPLE

I am aware from one of our mediumship enquirers that she had a life as one of a group of visitors to Earth from another planet in 508BC. I will describe this in some detail to illustrate the outside influences on man's development. Today, she is incarnated as a human, but at that time she incarnated on another planet but visited Earth. Her group came therefore in their own form, which was not greatly unlike that of humans visually, just varied in some minor ways, although it differed somewhat internally. They radiated an aura that was more visible than that of humans and their colouring, hair eyes and skin was more intense, hence the populace elevating them to the position of gods.

At the time of 508BC, the Roman Republic was at its zenith. It is no accident that such an advanced classical civilisation occupied our planet at such a time. The planet on which the visitors were at that time incarnated had for some time been visiting Earth and were in the throes of a project to assist in the advancement of the planet's evolution and spirituality. They found Earth more backward in this respect than had been realised but with the sensitivity and spirituality of these people, no attempt was made to force their culture and beliefs on to the occupants of Earth, no attempt to colonize or control. The knowledge, the skills and advanced ways were taught to the populace, introduced and then allowed to germinate and grow in a way that could be accepted as natural for the planet. The Romans, however, with their lack of understanding, turned these visitors into Gods created mythology surrounding them and the planet from which they came. The nearest the earthly pronunciation of the planet's name one could come to was in our modern day language "Olympus". You can see what occurred, a whole "religion", a mythology built up around these visitors, which was not at all their intention.

They monitored the situation on Earth for some time, and then decided that the planet was not yet ready to absorb all that they could give it, that it would be too much, too soon. As their wish was to assist by enriching evolution and spiritual growth, not to change the course of the planet's evolution by giving the inhabitants the skills to become more effectively warlike and controlling, the project ceased, and no further knowledge was introduced at that time. As we know, Rome's power waned, and the advancement it and other classical civilisations had enjoyed slowed pace and in some cased reverted to the natural evolution that man could achieve unaided.

The skills brought by these visitors were the skills of building and architecture, of mathematics, science and invention. Philosophy and intellectual skills. Skills of healing and spirituality, skills of communication. Artistic and creative skills. They advanced the knowledge of the planet in all of these fields. In some cases the knowledge has been lost again. They would have continued with further lessons of technology and science and much more on the interaction of the incarnated and spiritual forms, but found the planet backward and warlike. They were appalled to find the human population took the new-found skills and used them for the purpose of conquer and control. This was not the idea. The project was to advance evolution and spiritual evolution, not to provide the means for a more effective form of barbarism. The project was deemed to be too much, too soon and so it was discontinued at that time. Some of the skills fell into disuse and diminished or disappeared. Others continued at the planet's own rate of development.

These were a gentle and spiritual people, their planet long ago having worked through the kindergarten stage of Earth. They would not have a concept of human, or any other type of sacrifice. I am afraid that invention was completely human! Another misconception of teachings from another race of visitors.

The particular lady whose past-life enquiry gave rise to me receiving this information of a life in 508BC was one of what we would call inspectors, with the task of observing and reporting on the progress of the race. They came as incarnated beings from another world. It was a journey undertaken by an incarnated being, just like a person from England journeying to America. The race they came from was extremely spiritual, had greater knowledge and spiritual communication and was far more evolved that the people of Earth, but they were incarnated beings, not spirit beings.

The role of inspector was a job of work like any other. Just like being an officer in the armed forces on Earth, a missionary, or a teacher. The life would have been planned in spirit, just like any other life. Spirit Council would not have had any involvement in it any more than it would in any life-plan. The position of inspector was an administrative role more than any other. Inspectors would be required to report on the progress of the race, report on the success or otherwise of the project. Others would have the roles of teachers, advisors and introducers of the knowledge. The reports would be delivered back to those in charge of the project on the home planet.

The project to advance life on Earth, to improve spirituality, was a project conceived and carried out by the incarnated beings of that world. Being far more spiritual, their desire to work for others' spiritual advancement was far greater than it would be elsewhere, but it was still the project of incarnated beings. They were greatly skilled in spiritual communication and could refer to spirit for guidance in their endeavours, could check that they were on the path, so to speak, but they were still incarnated beings with freewill choices. Undertaking this project would have been planned by them in spirit, but they when incarnated would carry it out. It is true to say that in their world, spirit nearly always achieved the goals of the lifetime because of the open flow of communication with spirit thirds, but choices could still occur, choices which would be different to any we would be presented with on Earth.

Space does not permit a discussion about other ancient civilisations. Some have been the subject of many books and theories and are well known – Ancient Egypt and the Mayan civilisation for instance. Some we discover only now, the city on

49

the bed of the Gulf of Khambhat, for instance, reported in the press in February 2002. I have discussed the evolution of planets in chapter one. Once inhabited by the most advanced variety of spirit, the time spent being the Nursery World is marked by rapid changes. The reason for the explosion in man's scientific progress from around 7500BC onwards with the initial development of agriculture and fixed homes instead of nomadic communities, is the arrival here of the variety of spirit of which we are a part. The reason why the graph has gone almost vertical in the twentieth century is a catch-up at the end of a nursery stage. Mobile phones, computers and the internet are the artefacts to re-accustom us to communication instantly with others elsewhere; something which some of our spiritual cultures, the Australian Aborigines for example, have never lost, yet whom many in the West disdain because of their lack of science! To go onward, the world now needs to go backward and regain its spirituality.

There are many abilities not yet developed by humans. Examples are thought transference and our healing skills. There is much knowledge yet to be given to us, which will be given when the time is judged correct and is scheduled in the greater plan. We have separated our thinking (as was intended) into the scientific and the spiritual. The way forward is for the two to come together again as they have in the ascent of man in the past. I now look at more of the detail of the mechanism how knowledge arrives here: the role of the spirit guide, and spirit communication. The best evidence of the guide at work is "synchronicity", and I give illustrations of that too.

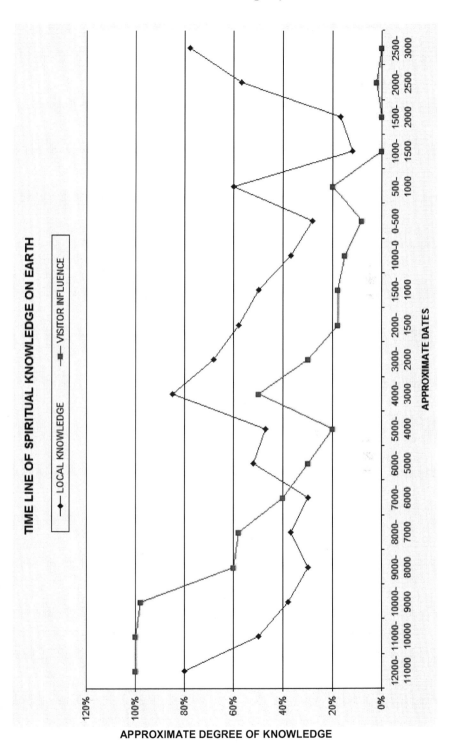

EXPLANATION OF TIME LINE

APPROXIMATE YEAR	**EVENT**
12000BC	ATLANTIS
10000BC	ARRIVAL OF HOMO SAPIENS ON EARTH, AGRICULTURE BEGINS
4500BC	TANG-SHO CULTURE IN CHINA
3500BC – 2300BC	SUMERIAN CIVILISATION, MINOAN CIVILISATION MENES IN EGYPT - RING OF BRODGAR
2000 – 1000BC	PAGANS, DRUIDS, CELTS, PHOENICIANS AND MYCENAEANS
800BC – 146BC	GREEK CIVILISATION BEGINS AGAIN AFTER A PERIOD OF DARK AGE
753BC – AD476	ANCIENT ROME
0	CHRISTIANITY BEGINS
AD1119 – 1314	KNIGHTS TEMPLAR
AD2000	WHERE WE ARE TODAY
AD2000 – 2500	WHERE WE SHOULD BE IN THE NEXT 500 YEARS
AD2500 – 3000	WHERE WE SHOULD BE BY THE END OF THE MILLENNIUM

Definition of Spiritual Knowledge: Awareness of the spirit dimension, ability to communicate, knowledge of earth energies and how to use them.

SCIENCE AND SPIRIT

> *"I make bold to claim that almost every boon in your world,
> every invention, and every discovery has its origin in the
> realms of spirit. The minds of your world are but the
> receptacles of the greater minds who use them to confer new
> benefits to your world of matter.*
>
> *"You are executing plans which you have helped to create and
> bring about in your own world. All the original work, if you
> like to use those words, is done in our world because all the
> energising, all the dynamic, originates not with matter but
> with spirit."*
>
> Silver Birch: "The Universe of Silver Birch"

This part of this chapter attempts to explain how all scientific
progress is either spirit inspired or spirit directed. To do so, I will
look at what thought is, some of the ways spirit communication
takes place, and the sources of knowledge. The phenomenon
known as synchronicity is our clue to spotting how we are guided
along, in the case of scientists, a path of discovery.

As a consequence of the Enlightenment movement of the
seventeenth and eighteenth centuries, Western thought moved
away from religious ideologies and ways of interpreting the world,
to become the farthest ever removed from spiritual concepts.
Those concepts as explained are not to be confused with religions.
As many are aware, religions are manmade and have become
characterised by control, dogma and ritual. The existence of life-
plans is why Robert Musil was accurate when he wrote, *"It is not
true that the scientist goes after truth. It goes after him."* Life-
plans are a key concept in understanding what happens in life.

If one looks at human scientific progress in modern times, one can
detect some pattern in it. Firstly, it is usually a single individual,
not a committee or group that advances knowledge. Secondly,
they are Western, not third world or Chinese. The blueprint that
spirit uses in the introduction of new knowledge is, it is a task

chosen by a single older spirit, when that spirit is ready to undertake it. All spirit will be required at some point to introduce new knowledge to a place of incarnation. The timing has to fit in with the plan for the planet. The actual culture or society into which the individual incarnates will also be predetermined. The reason Britain was a powerhouse of inventions in the eighteenth and nineteenth centuries was because that was the nation intended to lead innovation in the planetary plan at that time.

THOUGHT

One of the tenets of Christianity is that thought originates with the soul. This science changed us into believing thought originates with the brain and that we have no soul! Religion in this instance is correct; all thought originates in the spirit or soul. What our brains do is give expression to thought, to select the words to put into language those thoughts, and then to operate the physical organs associated with speech. Thought is in fact, a vibration, hence the familiar experience of having just walked into a room and picking up an atmosphere when an argument has just taken place, or in the opposite case, when a peaceful or joyous experience has occurred, we sense the harmony.

Our experiences also demonstrate that thought travels, and indeed is capable of travel over long distances. Just as we send out our thoughts, so too do we receive them. Hence the quite common experience of knowing who is calling before we pick up the telephone to answer it. I personally experience a burning sensation in either left or right ear when someone is talking about me in strongly emotional terms. (This is usually, I believe, my ex-wife in my right ear even though I can be up to three hundred miles away from her at the time). What is happening is that our aura, the energy field that surrounds us, is registering receipt of the vibration and translating this into the burning ear feeling.

This experience is the early stages of a sixth sense, one which all humans are capable of developing but do not use yet. It is an early form of telepathy. Where two people have a very close bond, one that sometimes occurs in marriages but can also occur between two friends or two family members, they often can instinctively know the other's mood and feelings without the need for words. Sometimes actual thoughts are shared, which is further evidence of connection on a spiritual level. They are either soul mates (or "soul twins") or have shared many incarnations together and are therefore key members of what I term the same "soul group". What happens is the familiarity on the spiritual level allows the thought of one to be picked up by the other, or they may have the same thought simultaneously or with a small lapse of time.

The vibrations produced by thought have now been photographed using frozen water (Masaru Emoto *"Messages from Water"*). It is fascinating to see that the same word in different languages produces very similar patterns. In spirit, language is not necessary, hence not being bound by its limitations when we are in that dimension. Many now have captured spirit orbs in digital camera photos. These are spirit of the variety capable of incarnating as human. If one enlarges the photo, one can see an intricate pattern in the orb. This changes constantly with the thoughts of the spirit.

Have you ever wondered why we do not all sound exactly the same when we speak? There are, of course, regional accents and so on but when, for example, children in a classroom recite poetry, being similar in biological age and most likely from the same district, why would the teacher be able to identify the speaker by their voice were she unable to see the class? If one way children learn language is by mimicking their parents, why do they not sound exactly like their mother or father? The answer is that each spirit or soul has its own unique vibration and when a spirit makes a thought and then vocalises it, the spirit's unique vibration comes through in the voice.

COMMUNICATION

Although it is not yet common for two incarnated spirits to be able to communicate telepathically, each of us is in communication at various times with our spirit guide, the other part of our energy that remains behind in the spirit dimension. What very few of us are trained to do is recognise communication when we receive it, hence it passes unnoticed for what it is. In everyday language we speak of "instinct" or "intuition" or "gut feeling". What these often are, in fact, are the most noticeable instances of communication from the spirit guide, whose role it is to get us to achieve our life-plan, to get us in the right place at the right time to allow our destiny to develop, subject to our free-will choice whether we follow the plan or not.

In older spirit, the communication ability is often more finely honed and hence not limited to moments of intuition, but can occur over a longer period of time and with clarity. This is the phenomenon known as "channelling", direct communication with one's spirit guide. This can be done consciously or unconsciously. An example of the former is "trance mediumship", where a guide takes over the body and speaks through an incarnated person. At the same time, the person's voice often changes and actual appearance may do so. (The guide projects his or her persona onto the medium's aura so it looks as if physical identity has changed). This can be fascinating to witness, but there is no need for the guide to go to that extreme. It is easier to connect at the thought level. Many mediums when giving what is termed "readings" often are merely the mouthpiece for messages from the enquirer's spirit guide. It looks and sounds as if it is the medium speaking but what is happening is the medium's guide and own energy have become one for the purpose of delivering the thoughts. Those thoughts originate with the enquirer's guide, which are then relayed through the medium's guide who vocalises them using the medium's body.

We all have the potential to have conscious communication with our guide. Examples of this happening on an unconscious level are when we have premonition experiences, the guide showing us something just before it happens, and being able to make prescient remarks, again the guide telling us the future, this time in words not pictures. What many people may be familiar with, but not know it for what it is, is the instance of making a witty, or knowledgeable remark and quite surprising oneself with the speed of delivery and afterwards thinking "did I really just say that?", or "that was a clever remark". This may well have been our spirit guide speaking through us.

Now if we look at certain great people of the past, such as Michelangelo, Leonardo da Vinci, Shakespeare or Mozart, those who have advanced civilisation, culture and the arts in some significant way, then we will find they have three things in common. They were older spirits, their life-plans called for them to create artistic works that would influence many others, and they had clear communication with their spirit guide. Those who watched the film *"Amadeus"*, for example, may recall Salieri's envy and wonder at how Mozart could write such perfect scores without the need for correction. Shakespeare's first publisher reported, "His hand and mind went together". What these two examples illustrate is the help of the spirit guide in creating their masterpieces (together with past-life skill in their discipline). In effect, their works were channelled if not wholly, then certainly in part. Mozart would not have known he had guide communication as the reason he found it easy to write his music. *"Everything has been composed but not yet written down"*, he once wrote to his father. Shakespeare, on the other hand, was aware of hearing his guide.

Channelling is one method of direct communication. Another is meditation. Indeed for anyone wishing to meet their spirit guide or to improve conscious interaction with their higher self, meditation is the best means of doing so. The famous English scientist, Isaac Newton, a cofounder of the Enlightenment Movement and regarded as an icon and almost god-like figure for a period, explained that he used meditation as the means to obtaining his discoveries. His biographer John Maynard Keynes remarked on his "unusual powers of continuous concentrated introspection". By going within ourselves and seeking the guide's help, we can uncover great wisdom.

One can puzzle how was it that an obscure young man called Albert Einstein working in the Swiss patent office, no academic institution, produced in 1905 a paper that solved several of the deepest mysteries of the universe. This was his Special Theory of Relativity. C P Snow wrote that it was as if Einstein "had reached the conclusions by pure thought, unaided, without listening to the opinions of others. To a surprisingly large extent that is precisely what he had done". What C P Snow did not appreciate was the help Einstein would have had from his spirit guide. It would have been a combination of various communications. When Einstein famously remarked, *"imagination is more important than knowledge"*, what he was referring to was spirit communication, had he known consciously that is why his imagination was so powerful. One example that we all experience is "night teachings". That is, we are given information in our sleep state which we rarely recall consciously, but often we can "just know" something during the day. Another example is actually going to sleep with questions on our mind and then first thing in the morning, before fully awake, hearing the answers from our guide. Most people believe our brains have worked on the questions overnight to be the reason we obtain the solution. That is true, but not a complete explanation. Largely unrecognised, we receive much and regular communication whilst asleep.

Guides will only give the answers if it assists the life-plan, just in case you wonder why we all did not write the Theory of Relativity. In composing a life-plan, sometimes one will repeat a skill or occupation. Thus talent or genius is explained by the fact one has refined that skill in earlier lives. We all experience reincarnation and in fact only spend a small proportion of our lives on Earth. Einstein was clearly an exceptional human. Spiritually, part of the explanation is that he had not previously had a life here. Very few of us have not had a previous life here, some of us have had very many. All his past lives were spent on what I term E T (extraterrestrial) worlds, many of which were more advanced than here.

It is possible to enhance spirit communication by being on an energy site. This is most commonly found as ley lines. What these are is a subtle change in the earth's magnetic field caused by the flow of "universal energy". This arrives from the stars and is quite distinct from light. It is the life-force, without which no life can exist, and all life by definition contains this energy. One inventor who used it to aid his link with his guide was Marconi. He revolutionised human communication by developing radio transmission over long distances. His first successful transatlantic transmission in 1901 was from Pollhu in Cornwall to

Newfoundland. That spot in Cornwall is on a strong ley line known as the Apollo line.

Marconi's life-plan included the making of a dramatic technological leap. He actually knew of the increased thought processes to be had at certain places where he felt "vibrations" within himself. He did not realise what these were and did not realise the new thoughts he experienced in these places came from his guide, but he had identified the fact that there were these special places where he felt different and then received sudden "brainwaves" that moved his work on apace. In time he came to seek out such places to assist him, but he never shared this thought with others, preferring to keep his own counsel on the subject.

My personal experience of thought travelling and guide communication is noticing the occasions I answer a question in a talk before it has been asked. A person in the audience may think of a question, their guide "hears" it, then sends it to my guide, who then channels the answer and I speak it. I do not know why I say the information, it just comes to mind. A person may then say, *"I was going to ask you that"*, or *"You have answered something that has puzzled me"*, and I just smile knowingly.

KNOWLEDGE

All is known in the spirit dimension, all history of all planets, the future of all planets and all laws of physics and matter, much of which we have as a race yet to discover. All planets have a development plan and new information is only given to us when the time is right and so appropriate for the planet's stage of development.

At the risk of damaging our egos, I regret to repeat that Earth is known as the "nursery world" of the universe. We are the starting off world for the highest variety of spirit. There are many civilisations far more advanced spiritually and technologically than we are. If we have reached our present state of knowledge in a mere 10,000 years imagine a civilisation 100,000 years old and its state of development. Many of those incarnating on Earth are also older spirit. They come back to be teachers or to advance knowledge or the arts in some way. All of us suffer temporary amnesia on arrival here from the spirit dimension so do not consciously recall our past lives and the spirit state, but we do bring subconscious memories through sometimes and these can be the basis of what we consider acts or moments of genius. Alternatively, such acts are instances of prompting and help from our spirit guide, perhaps a recall of a past life incarnation where the invention was in use. Many of our advances in electronics and space travel, for example, are in fact knowledge introduced from more advanced civilisations through an incarnation here of a spirit that has previously experienced that knowledge elsewhere.

Many may have noticed the technological acceleration of the last century. What has happened is a period of "catch up" has been taking place. Earth has fallen behind in what is regarded as the appropriate technological knowledge for its point of development, so it has been arranged more spirit incarnate with life-plans that include the advancement of science and applied knowledge. To go from first flight to man on the moon in seventy years is indeed a wonder given the previous millennia when travel was nothing more advanced than riding on a horse's back or walking. A wonder that is, until one is aware, the speeding up was prompted by those spirit responsible for overseeing the evolution of Earth because the end of a cycle of evolution was approaching with the year 1999.

SPIRIT COUNCIL

In greatly simplified terms, the connection between each one of us, God and the overseeing spirit, is that all consists of energy and the life-force, which is found everywhere in the universe. Each one of us is a soul or spirit that has broken away from the Source (Higher Power, Collective, Great Spirit or God being alternative terms) to undertake a journey of experiences. When fulfilled, the enriched spirit returns back to the Source taking this enrichment with it. Certain older spirit when nearing completion of their experiences, are invited onto a Council, a body of spirit that supervises the evolution of all planets, including Earth.

The spirit that was Einstein is a member of Spirit Council as are those that were Darwin and Freud. (Incidentally, the latter failed in his life-plan. He overplayed the importance of the sex drive in his work. The intention was to show us the complexities of the mind.) What distinguishes an old spirit incarnation from one that is Council directed is that the latter is intended to impact on how man sees himself as well as advancing knowledge. Few incarnations by Council members are world-changing. Some are what may be termed "fact finding" or just completing their personal experiences. Spirit Council has been referred to as the "brethren of Christ", but that is the result of trying to make new knowledge fit the existing religious framework. Other high profile past incarnations of its members include Nostradamus and Shakespeare, and of course the most famous of all spiritual master incarnations, Jesus. He is a Council member, but not a special one, except that he is a member of the Administrative Council, which oversees other parts of that body.

Certain members of the Council form "sub-committees" as it were, for certain tasks. One, for example, is tasked with the design and introduction of new species. Another is concerned with technological progress for use by the highest variety of spirit, which on Earth is the one incarnating as human. (Other spirit varieties incarnate on Earth within their species, namely mammal, bird, fish, insect, reptile.) We think of scientific advancement and inventions as the product of human genius. They are, but behind that genius is spirit direction. The ultimate source of new inventions will either be from Spirit Council, relayed through a spirit guide to his or her incarnated other part, or an incarnated spirit "remembering" the artefact or device from a previous life on another planet. A third possibility is visitors from another planet, humanoid in appearance, bringing new knowledge.

As explained, this happened with our ancient civilisations and explains, in part, why Ancient Egyptian, Ancient Greek and Roman civilisations were able to take huge leaps forward compared with what had gone before and in such a relatively short space of time. A modern day individual example is the great Victorian engineer, Isambard Kingdom Brunel. His achievements were leading edge projects – docks, bridges, tunnels, ships. His remembrance of technology elsewhere is illustrated by his attempt to introduce a vacuum railway. It was an idea too soon – the materials to make it work properly were not yet here, but he had an inner knowledge that such an idea should work!

It is not just technology advances but architectural ones that are "imported". Am I alone in thinking our Gothic cathedrals are not a design that originated here? Certain aspects of them have a distant familiarity which is because I have experienced the architecture on another world. Some modern developments too, can seem "déjà vu" in style. The most startling of these is perhaps some in the Gulf, in particular those of Nakheel in Dubai. These manmade islands of homes built on poles in the shape of a palm are described as *"visionary"*. They are similar to those found on the planet Atlantis, the architect's source of inspiration from past lives there. I was momentarily transfixed when I saw an aerial picture of one of them, the Palm, Deira. I could not believe I was seeing something on Earth so other-worldly.

THE FUTURE KNOWN

A demonstrable example of scientific advancement being knowledge already known elsewhere is the discovery of the shape of the DNA compound, the component of chromosomes and genes. Watson and Crick are credited with the discovery of the double helix in 1953, later to receive a Nobel Prize. Rosslyn chapel near Edinburgh is a storehouse in stonework of secret coded Knights Templar knowledge built in 1446. One of its most impressive stone carvings is named the Apprentice Pillar. When I saw it on a visit in 2001, I had the immediate thought, the mason had represented the DNA double helix in his work. It is in fact, a quadruple helix but which I had interpreted to be both sides of the pillar having the double one. I asked my guide about it.

The apprentice concerned in the carving of the pillar at Rosslyn had incarnated on another world where the humanoid life-form carried its own form of DNA, the quadruple helix he later inscribed on the pillar. He worked in the field of genetics in this other world and had deep level memory of it. This pattern was within his very essence of being. He had a desperate need to imprint it somewhere for posterity, without understanding the reason for this need within him. It was his destiny to leave it for future discovery at the risk of the wrath of his master in doing this. I am further told the full implications of it will not be understood for some many years yet.

Subsequent work to the discovery of the double helix by scientists has led to the puzzling observation that almost half of human genes (the largest proportion known in any organism) do not appear to have any purpose. Their sole function is merely to reproduce themselves! The spiritual answer is that the human body is what I describe in motor car terms, the "basic model". There are a number of abilities we have as a race yet to develop, with changes in our internal organs yet to take place, leading on to the "deluxe model". The genetic framework is in place awaiting the correct time in the planet's and human development plan for the "upgrades" to occur.

To show new knowledge comes from spirit, I will now make a further observation that science has yet to discover: the DNA blueprint for physical life is in our energy system, in our aura. This has to be so, for the foetus in the womb to develop and for the constant renovation and replacement of cells that must go on to keep the human body in a functioning state. Spirit is present in the womb from the moment of conception and leaves when last breath is drawn. The physical body would not have come into existence without the spiritual (or energy) blueprint upon which to hang and interlink itself. The implications of this for medicine are far-reaching. The future leaps in treatment of illness will be alternative, not mainstream. There will be denial and opposition before this observation will become accepted as is often the case with new knowledge.

My speaking of knowledge elsewhere is easily dismissed by the sceptic because science has not yet found other intelligent life in the universe. It is intended that life on Mars be discovered, but not yet. It is October 2004 at the time of writing. The discovery will be made in fifteen years time. It will be discovered that Mars once had an atmosphere and biological life. It will be further discovered, the loss of atmosphere was caused by the actions of the dominant life-form! This discovery will have an important role to play in the development of Earth, changes in the structure and hierarchy of how we govern ourselves. (This discovery will coincide in 2019 with the second opportunity, should the first one not occur in 2012, for Earth's vibration to take an upward change. I describe more of that in chapter five.)

PARADIGM SHIFT

Science is the intermediate phase between religion and spiritual truths. It has allowed knowledge of the physical world to flourish that would have been stifled and suffocated by religion. Yet science has its limits. How did language evolve? How is thought produced? Is there meaning to life beyond the reproduction of DNA? These are some of the questions it cannot answer, but which can be answered spiritually. Science is at its weakest when it attempts to explain the past. What is the origin of life? It was not spontaneous. What was the purpose of Stonehenge? It was not a "temple"! How and why were the Ancient Egyptian pyramids built? Not by human muscle cutting and hauling the blocks and not as tombs. The answers to these, and indeed any question, is known in the spirit dimension. To receive the answers one needs the permission of one's spirit guide and to have refined the skill to use our so-called sixth sense.

Most of the people on Earth are young spirits. They will not go on a search for life's meaning as it is not their time to do so. For the significant proportion here who are older spirit, that search is made so much more challenging by the Western rational-scientific culture. It is the way of nursery worlds (the status Earth currently has) that those who choose to incarnate onto them do so without knowledge (in the main) of their reason for being there or knowledge of the spirit that they are. Why would any spirit then choose to incarnate in such a place? The answer is the degree of progression that may be achieved from "climbing up the ladder of ignorance" that these worlds provide. In the case of higher evolved spirit, who will have led many spiritual lives, the challenge is great of being in this world of little spirituality without knowledge of one's spiritual self. Two paths emerge from this situation, one to accept the view of the masses, the other the carrying through to a sufficient degree the spirituality achieved prior to incarnation to cause the person to question the accepted ways.

The polarity that has grown up between the scientific and the spiritual was for the experiences it could provide. In other places spirit uses there is just knowledge, including the spiritual truths. On Earth, by way of contrast and challenge, the two have become separated, making the one more difficult to find for the scientist. Now is the time for the two to come together again so even greater discoveries than we have had so far can be made and man can live more in balance with himself and the planet. If the two do not come together then we have a Doomsday scenario – climate change, increased pollution, further depletion of natural resources, disease, famine and so on. It is a feature of human nature, that only when on the brink of disaster does man decide to do something and look for new ways of dealing with a problem. These will in fact be the old ways, waiting for him to rediscover.

The phenomenon of "synchronicity" or meaningful coincidences has played a significant part in major scientific discoveries. I use illustrations of this in relation to science in the next chapter, which I devote wholly to this subject of coincidence that shape our destiny if we spot them and act on them.

CHAPTER FOUR

SYNCHRONICITY

Introducing new knowledge is done by way of a task or challenge.
A person may need to spend years of research or trial and error,
before making his or her breakthrough. To aid us along the road
of discovery, spirit guides provide hints and clues in the
phenomenon that has been termed "synchronicity" or meaningful
coincidence. It is one of the ways of detecting the planned nature
of our lives. To return to my example of Isaac Newton, perhaps
the most famous of all illustrations of synchronicity, is his visit to
a fair at Stourbridge near Cambridge in 1664. At a stall selling all
manner of oddities he saw a prism, which he bought. This led him
to study light. Optics was one area in which he advanced
knowledge, showing us white light is in fact, a combination of
coloured light, which exists as a spectrum. He transformed our
understanding of light. This would have been part of his life-plan.
How does the guide get us to discover our plan? There are many
possible subtleties, synchronicity being one, and one instance of
synchronicity can be making a seemingly small and
inconsequential purchase that in fact turns out to be a hidden
pointer to destiny.

The purchase of the prism was the spark to ignite a drive to study
light. That drive would be within Newton because he was
subconsciously aware of his life-plan, or it was the influence of his
spirit guide, or a combination of the two. A similar synchronicity
had occurred the previous year. Newton, at the same fair, had
bought a book on astrology. He did not understand the maths in
it, which triggered him to read books on maths. Until that time he
had not studied maths but henceforth developed a deep interest,
which culminated in the publication of his world-famous book,
"Principia", that included his three famous laws of motion. That
was his major task, which he very nearly did not accomplish,
having spent almost two decades on research, analysis and side
issues, needing to be prompted by Halley in 1684 to do so, another
synchronicity which was an "engineered" meeting of the two.

All our lives on Earth will contain many instances of synchronicity. Most, if not all, will have passed unnoticed as such; some will have been missed completely. If we trace backwards to the small acts of coincidence that precede a major turning point in our lives, we can discover them. In the case of our famous scientists and inventors, synchronicity will often be found linked to their discoveries. For example, there are two associated with the discovery of radioactivity. Henri Becquerel in Paris in 1896 just happened to have "carelessly left a packet of uranium salts on a wrapped photographic plate in a drawer". The salts were found later to have burned an impression on the plate. A second instance of synchronicity then occurred. He did not investigate the important finding himself, but passed it to a graduate student. That student was a Polish émigré, Marie Curie, who went on to make further discoveries and coined the term "radioactivity", to describe the effect. Clearly it was not in his life-plan to do so, but to be the facilitator; he did jointly receive a Nobel prize in physics with the Curies.

Synchronicity can also be the actions of guides of third parties to help us along a pathway. To give an illustration of this, let us take a critical point in Charles Darwin's life. It was his life-plan to discover the evidence to support the theory of evolution. It had been pre-planned in spirit that he would visit the Galapagos Islands, because of the unique flora and fauna there, that would lead him to make his profound revelations. First of all the British Government had to decide to send a ship on a circumnavigation voyage, (largely for mapping the coastline, not scientific purposes). Secondly the Captain (and others) suggested a companion for conversation on the long voyage and so the decision to take a scientist was made, but this was very much a subsidiary reason. Darwin was one of three people invited. The position was unpaid, so Darwin needed his father's financial support. His father opposed the idea, so he wrote a letter reluctantly declining, unable to go against his father's view. The world was not going to hear of Charles Darwin it seemed. Then synchronicity occurred! The two others who had both initially wanted to accept, declined the invitation, and Darwin's uncle helped change his father's attitude. This outcome was, of course, the guides at work "behind the scenes". Guides cooperate with each other in getting the person in the right place at the right time, to move the pieces on the chessboard of life. In the words of Shakespeare, the human actors, *"they have their exits and entrances"* on life's stage, the guides acting as director in this.

Why, you may ask, does spirit proceed by uncertain synchronicity and not, say, by red and green lights made highly visible? The answer is we would not otherwise create "the game of life". Anyone who enjoys spectator sports would no doubt confirm that if you knew the final score or outcome in advance, it takes away the excitement of uncertainty of the result whilst the game is in progress. Another reason for synchronicity is the spiritual growth possible in being able to spot a destiny, even if this is not done on a conscious level. This occurs at what I have termed "crossroads" situations, where the life-path can go one of two ways. However, synchronicity is necessary to arrive at those crossroads or major decision points, so the two are often interlinked.

Where two people arrive at the same scientific breakthrough at around the same time, this will also be spiritually intended. Because of freewill, one person may not introduce the knowledge intended, so a "back up" or contingency life is arranged. This happened for example with the Theory of Evolution. Both Darwin and Wallace arrived at the same theory of natural selection, Wallace in case Darwin did not succeed. He arrived at it in a "flash of insight" in 1857 and corresponded with Darwin. He was used as a prompt to get Darwin to publish (synchronicity again!), who had sat on his manuscript for thirteen years since 1844. The nineteenth century thinker Ralph Waldo Emerson, explained this coincidence by saying ideas were *"in the air"*. In the next century, Jung came closer with his concept of *"universal unconsciousness"*. To be more specific, the explanation is a combination of world plans, life-plans, spirit guides and synchronicity.

The latter is such an evidential phenomenon for the workings of spirit, that I would like to write in more detail about it. *"There is divinity in odd numbers, either in nativity, chance or death"* wrote Shakespeare. This seems an absurd remark, or strange humour perhaps, unless one has knowledge of the spiritual reference he so succinctly described, that of synchronicity. Let us further examine his choice of words and the spiritual concept of synchronicity or "chance".

ODD NUMBERS

These do have a significance that even numbers do not. Odd numbers are the equivalent of a positive charge, and even a negative one. We all know electricity flows from positive to negative. Similarly, there is an attraction between numbers, or rather the energy configuration that is represented by numbers. The special significance of odd numbers by their association with divinity includes the following:

ONE -   Symbolises the One, Unity, the Source and so on.

THREE -   A powerful number, being the spiritual three or trinity. Each soul or spirit on its journey subdivides into three parts.

FIVE -   The spiritual journey consists of five levels.

SEVEN -   Each of those levels is subdivided into seven stages. There are seven planes in the spirit dimension. Universal energy, the life-force found everywhere, has seven "life" components. There are seven levels within a life plan.

NINE -   There are nine (not seven) principal chakras in the human aura, which has nine layers to it. There are nine components of universal energy in total.

I interpret Shakespeare's use of *"divinity"* as shorthand for the spirit dimension and the workings of it. There are many philosophies that discuss the significance and representation of numbers. I have no wish to contradict them, but to give my explanation of the connection between divinity and odd numbers. Connection exists between language and numbers, the universal life-force and numbers and personality and numbers, which are beyond the scope of this book. I discuss numbers linked with events.

The famous English scientist, Isaac Newton, had a life-plan to show us the mathematics governing the motions of heavenly bodies. He showed us these were not chaotic but ordered; that there are universal laws. The existence of those laws implied also, the existence of a Creator. Odd numbers are themselves a big clue to realising the design to existence, both individual life-stories and that of world events, and also the timing of events in personal lives and that of the planet. The repeated feature of certain numbers is beyond any random statistical explanation. Like Newton's discoveries, it tells us a divinity or providence is involved.

To give an illustration, when composing an individual life-plan and in making one for a planetary cycle, the number three and its multiples are often used in the timing of certain events and as a feature of them. Perhaps the most momentous example of timing is the fact that World War Two began on the third day of the ninth month of the thirty-ninth year of the century. The same third day of the ninth month had been used previously. Oliver Cromwell won two of his most decisive battles in the English Civil War on the third of September, the battle of Dunbar against the Scots in 1650 and a year later, against an invading army at Worcester. He also died on that day in 1658.

Examples of three and its multiples which feature in events are: the number of days fighting in the Falklands war was thirty-three; the number of scud missiles fired by Iraq in the 1991 Gulf war was thirty-nine; there were sixty-six hostages taken by students in 1980 in Teheran, their disastrous rescue attempt a feature in President Carter's failure to be re-elected.

In the world plan, one can see the number three has a preference. For example, the opposing European powers at the outbreak of World War One in 1914, were either members of the Triple Alliance or the Triple Entente; Bismark, in the previous century, had unified Germany and fought and won three wars in doing so; the Romans had fought three Punic Wars; mainland UK is currently composed of three countries; the English constitution consists of three parts, Sovereign, Lords and Commons; our education system is divided largely into three, primary, secondary and further education; *"All Gaul is divided into three parts"* was the first line translation of a Latin textbook I suffered at school! Three and its multiple is not universal, but its frequency as a feature in timing or as component, is more than randomness or chance would suggest.

I would now like to give an illustration of the use of three in an individual life-plan, my own, as a case study. When we plan a life to come, we know in outline the major world events that are to happen and if we wish, can chose the timing of our birth to be able to participate in one or more of those events. This is true in my case. My year of birth is 1952. This was not chosen for its own sake, but because it predates by sixty years, a most important year in Earth's calendar. The year 2012 is intended to be the first opportunity for the planet's vibration to move upwards. It is an exciting time spiritually, known as the Point of Change, when a planet loses its "nursery" status and moves to a higher cycle. Wishing to experience that, I chose to be born sixty years beforehand. Why so long you ask? That is because I chose the first fifty years as a conventional material life, years of preparation, leading up to a year for change, that of 2002. I then intended to spend ten years living and working spiritually as part of the build-up to 2012.

To further explain the year 2002, there are certain years known in spirit as "wake-up" years. They occur every seven years. 1995 was one and 2002 is the latest. These are years when we sometimes plan traumatic experiences for ourselves, those experiences designed to shake our complacency and comfort and perhaps start us off on a new direction. There is thus some spiritual basis to the saying, "seven year itch". 1995 was not the seventh year of my marriage, but was the year of its collapse.

I suffered other personal traumas in 1995, three in total, would you believe! These set me off on a spiritual quest, part of their intended purpose. By my marriage I had three children. I am now experiencing my third long-term relationship and as this is

71

now with my soul-mate, it is planned to be the last. The year 2002 also marked the eighteenth year I had been self-employed. It was the intended year for change, but in 2001 I couldn't wait any longer and sold my house and business, although remaining a part-owner of it until 2002. Actually by doing this, I jumped the gun and missed out on things intended by the sale of the property in 2002, which can now be seen with hindsight.

Sixty, three, three, eighteen, we can see the bias towards three and its multiples that I used in my life-plan, also my linking it to a world event and to years for change which occur every seven years. There is a divinity in odd numbers!

NATIVITY

Contrary to some opinions, no pregnancy is accidental or unintended. To qualify that statement let me say, whether the pregnancy involves a miscarriage, abortion or going to term will not be chance, although it may be unplanned or unwanted on a human level. Spiritually, all pregnancies are intended events, and where not resulting in a live birth, those too will be planned for the experiences of the mother, the foetus, or both, as a spirit is present from the moment of conception.

The number of children we have is pre-planned before incarnation, but not always the actual spirit that takes on the role of our children. If this role is to be filled by one's soul-mate or a key member of the soul group it may be planned, but otherwise this is one of the tasks of the spirit guide. The guide will "audition" potential children to see if their plans and those of the parents are going to lead to the experiences chosen by both.

We can look at one aspect of nativity, date of birth, and sometimes see synchronicity, which we cannot in the event itself. Sometimes a day of birth can be selected in a life-plan to alert the person to their special significance. That featured in Isaac Newton's life. Being born on Christmas day fuelled his vanity, causing him to believe he was somehow singled out. He was, but not in any religious saviour sense.

Sometimes we use the birth or death day and month of a life we intend to copy in some manner. For example, the little known Spanish composer Arriaga was born on the same day as Mozart, 27th January, but exactly fifty years later. In life he knew little or nothing of Mozart, but his musical style is almost indistinguishable from his famous predecessor. His life has other similarities too.

Stephen Hawking, the famous Cambridge scientist, shares the same day for his birth as the death exactly three hundred years earlier of the great Italian mathematician and astronomer, Galileo Galilei, 8th January. It would be incorrect in fact to assume one was the reincarnation of the other, but a natural one given their parallel lives in maths and science. The reason it would be incorrect is because we choose variety along the spiritual journey and being famous is only given to us once, but we all have our fifteen minutes of fame somewhere along the path.

Like Arriaga with Mozart's life, the spirit that is currently Stephen Hawking, I suspect, planned his life modelled to some extent on that earlier life of the pioneering scientist, Galileo. This is not cheating; we can use predecessor lives for ideas and inspiration if we wish. One has a feeling of a malicious fate when seeing the outstanding brain in an incapacitated body that is the apparent misfortune of Stephen Hawking. It is not so, but part of his courageous life-plan. Being such a high profile scientist has set an excellent teaching example to the rest of us, that disability of the body does not mean incapacity of the brain! So many of us view someone in a wheelchair as unable to think and speak for themselves, treating physical disability as a mental condition as well.

Sometimes a child will have the same birthday as a parent. This usually results in the intended closer bond between the child and one parent. I have no evidence of this in the case of John Lennon, the assassinated pop star, but he is an example. He was born on 9th October, so was his son. In fact, there were many synchronicities in his life involving the number nine. He recognised the frequency of it, but not the significance. It was so arranged by his guide to show him the planned nature of his life.

The many instances have been recorded by his biographer, Ray Coleman.

No doubt one can see coincidence by looking hard or long enough. The difficult part is to distinguish between just a coincidence and a "significant" or spiritually intended one. For example, my own birthday is 10th April, 1952. This coincides with exactly forty years since the maiden voyage of the "*Titanic*". Not just a coincidence perhaps, when I reveal I have had a life-long interest in ships and the sea. I have written chapter six to explain the tragedy in spiritual terms, including the synchronicity linked with the "accident". I have never felt a fascination with the ship, however, nor ever been on board an ocean-liner. It is just a coincidence therefore, since there is no link with my life-story, unlike the examples of Arriaga and Stephen Hawking with their coincidental birth dates.

DEATH

There is divinity in the timing of one's death. The approximate time will be in the person's life-plan. They may have chosen year and even month sometimes. Thus, when we see someone dying young in tragic circumstances, we do not realise it was so planned. The late Princess Diana is an example. She chose to die aged thirty-six. She was aware of her life-plan to some extent in expressing her fears over a car accident before it happened. She died on 31st August, which leads me to suspect she had chosen the month of September in her life-plan, but that circumstances presented themselves in late August. She was similar to Mozart in choosing the age thirty-six, as did my brother.

When a spirit has achieved the experiences intended or indeed, as part of those experiences, a guide will "help" in arranging an exit. For example, the late Christopher Reeve, the former "*Superman*" actor who tragically became quadriplegic and then a high profile campaigner for the disabled, died from a cause that normally would not be fatal. He suffered a bedsore, which became infected and led to a subsequent heart attack, this being the cause of death. He had been quadriplegic for ten years. His death during the 2004 USA presidential election campaign was not coincidental.

He had campaigned against President Bush who opposed stem cell research in contrast to his opponent, John Kerry. It was judged by his guide, time to go. The timing of his death made stem cell research and the rights of the disabled, even more high profile issues.

The reader may be aware as I am, of an instance or instances of an elderly person having an injury as a result of a slip or fall. The trauma itself may not have been fatal, but was the start of a rapid deterioration in health, leading to demise. That trip or fall may not have been the "accident" it appears but spirit assisted, as it was judged by the person's guide the time to depart.

Conversely, there can be divinity in not dying when it seemed highly likely, or indeed, actually dying and being revived. These, too, are instances of the guide at work. There is the infamous life of Adolf Hitler to illustrate the guardian angel situation. He was one of only two persons in his regiment who began World War One in 1914 and was alive at the end of it. Some biographers have remarked on Hitler's apparent sixth sense, particularly when danger threatened him. Eyewitness accounts of fellow soldiers in that war speak of his ability to know, often within seconds, precisely where a shell would explode. In later years, he remarkably survived two bomb attempts on his life.

On 9th November 1939, he unaccountably cut short a speech in Munich and left. Minutes later a bomb went off in the hall killing several people. In 1944 another bomb exploded in the famous plot on his life by certain army generals. At the last moment the briefcase was moved away by a subordinate, so Hitler suffered minor injuries unlike others whose injuries were serious or fatal.

Hitler's life, although hideous to us in human terms, had a major significance in the world plan. Spirit made a careful watch over his life to ensure he fulfilled his destiny, which was to lead millions to their fate in World War Two, thus providing many with the emotional experiences required to advance their spiritual journey. His surviving the 1939 bomb will have had more than one purpose. It further fuelled his belief in his destiny, so emboldening him to make military decisions that proved so spectacularly successful. This over-confidence was also the seed of his undoing, when he later ignored the sound advice of his generals and made military blunders, also part of the plan.

There is also the contrary situation to Hitler, when for example, a leader is wounded or killed at a decisive moment, putting one side at a disadvantage. Historians have noticed how a "lucky shot" can have a disproportionate influence on the outcome of battles. An illustration is the Battle of Salamanca in 1812, when Wellington inflicted a significant defeat on the French in the Peninsular War. It marked a turning point, much as Stalingrad was to do in World War Two. As the English attack opened, the French commander, Marmont, was severely wounded by a British shell. His second in command was likewise put out of action. There was a twenty minute period during which the French had no commander. The outcome of all battles is known in spirit. One way the intended result is helped, is the "fluke shot" hitting a leader.

Hitler is a high profile example of one's guide (or "divinity" or "providence") at work to prevent premature death. It is not unusual for spirit to engineer the continuation of physical life in many ordinary lives. We are just not aware it happens, hearing only about the famous or infamous ones. One lady came to us at a psychic event and disclosed a close secret. She said she knew she had suffered a heart attack and died. She saw her spirit in the bathroom mirror, having left the body. The next thing was, she woke up back in her body in hospital. Her guide, with assistance from other spirit, had repaired her overworked heart and sent her back into the body because she had unfinished work to do. We relayed this information to her from her guide. Being spiritually aware, she had suspected herself that this is what had happened and was comforted to have the confirmation.

Before leaving this topic, I will discuss the place of grief in our experiences. Grief is a valid and necessary part of our life experiences. It is an aspect of love. We can suffer badly from it since we have forgotten the true nature of existence – there is no death of the spirit. The many excellent mediums who relay messages from departed loved ones are a main source of evidence and a route to that discovery for an increasing number of people.

In my current life, I had one sibling, a brother, tragically killed in a car "accident", aged thirty-six. I grieved for his loss, unaware at the time it was his life-plan to so leave. Besides mediumship demonstrations, we are given spiritual messages of a general nature increasingly in the mass media. For example, in the 2003 film "*Matrix Reloaded*", the character known as the Keymaker is shot and killed. His dying words to the other characters were "It was meant to be". He was aware of his own life-plan.

CHANCE

It will be no surprise to learn for those unfamiliar with his work, that synchronicity gave rise to psychologist Jung's modern-day pioneering investigations of synchronicity. The ancient Etruscans were one example of a civilisation very aware of synchronicity. This is explained by the fact that old spirit would have incarnated amongst them. The results of their observations concluded that the physical universe and everything in it are all interconnected by an unseen organising power.

Jung had an experience of what the Etruscans termed "ostenta". It was this: He was dealing with a troublesome case, a lady not susceptible to treatment because of her rigid beliefs and mind-set. She described a dream to him involving a golden scarab. At that very moment, Jung heard a tapping at the window. He saw it was an insect and opening the window, caught it as it flew inside. He gave it to his patient. It was a scarabaeid beetle, of gold-green colour. The woman's rationalistic mind-set was so shaken she was at last receptive to further treatment. No beetle had ever before or since, made such a noise at Jung's window, nor could he recollect seeing such a beetle so late in the season. What had brought about the amazing coincidental timing of this event, unbeknown to the participants, was the collusion between the patient's guide, Jung's guide and the spirit master responsible for overseeing insect life. They together had engineered the synchronicity.

How does synchronicity happen? All the thoughts we have as humans leave our mind and enter the spirit dimension. There they are all input together in what may be described as a "matrix".

As we are aware, there is the principle of cause and effect. When we think a thought, we give rise to the cause of an event happening. The effect is known in spirit, just before it happens in some cases. This is how the guide can intervene in "guardian angel" situations, for example, or those of the "lucky shot", mentioned earlier.

The mechanism whereby Hitler had a premonition of a shell exploding close by was this. The gunner firing the round thinks the thought of his intention to do so. This enters the "matrix". The result is calculated and his guide is alerted through his constant monitoring of his incarnated counterpart's thoughts entering the "matrix", that this event is going to impact on that person. He sends his immediate thought to the incarnated spirit to move out of the way, or even temporarily occupies his body and makes him move out of the way! Hence the seemingly miraculous escape. In Hitler's case, his survival of World War One was also intended in his life-plan to be the start of him thinking that he had a special destiny.

In the case of the lucky shot, the guides would either get the gunner to fire at precisely the moment firing would hit the target, or arrange the target to be in the spot the shell was known was going to fall, just before it did so. In the case of every battle in history, all the decision-takers would have additional spirit around them in addition to their main guide, helping the guide get the correct thinking in place for the intended result to occur. Hence, there are no happenstances in history, no great commanders nor stupid ones in a spiritual sense, but only in human terms.

Synchronicity is the act of our spotting a few of the many instances of the spirit guides at work, our clue to the organising spirit dimension, which surrounds us. We are not here by chance. The major events, circumstances and happenings in our own life are not random, contingent or accidental usually, but the result of a plan. The guide's role is to get us to achieve our plan, to get us in the right place at the right time, to bring us to what I term "crossroads" points, where we exercise our freewill choice to go one of two directions. All that takes a great deal of spirit engineering and cooperation between guides.

Can synchronicity be categorised? Frank Joseph in his book
"*Synchronicity and You*", identifies seventeen categories, the last
one of which he terms life-changing, or "transformational". The
first sixteen I regard as variations of either the guide saying
"hello" through a spotted coincidence, or the guide intending to
make the observer realise their life is not governed by mere
chance, the intention to be thought-provoking but not life-
changing. The repeat of a particular number is often used as
instance of synchronicity to draw attention to the mysteries of life,
as the example of John Lennon and the number nine.

To be in the category of "transformational", or what I would term
"meaningful coincidence", a synchronicity must have the character
of a signpost or a clue to the discovery of a destiny. That is only
deduced by what happens afterwards, by the chain of events
stemming from the synchronicity.

I have discussed elsewhere the spiritual references in the 1999
film "*The Matrix*", but I would like to use the film here, to
illustrate this type of synchronicity. The scriptwriters used two
references to "*Alice in Wonderland*" to help us spot it. The central
character, Neo, received an email he did not understand, which
was "*Follow the White Rabbit*". No explanation, no sender
identified, just that instruction. A short while later, a group of
people at his door includes a woman with a white rabbit tattoo on
her arm. Seeing his pallor and out of sorts mood, a member of the
group "spontaneously" invites him to a party to which they are en
route. Neo hesitates, his first thought is to decline, then on seeing
the tattoo, he accepts.

At this stage he still does not know the significance of the white
rabbit, if anything. He could choose to ignore the message, or fail
to see the woman's tattoo, as well as act upon it. Many intended
acts of synchronicity probably end up being missed, only the guide
knowing so, as it is so easy to let other thoughts and
considerations have precedence. Neo could very easily have
decided he was too tired to go out. The guide would then have
needed to set up another set of circumstances that formed

synchronicity. If at first we don't succeed,......... and so on.

At the party, Neo meets, completely unexpectedly, a woman named Trinity who unbeknown to him, is his soul-mate. Their conversation and initial meeting lead on to Neo's life being turned completely upside down. The meeting of his soul-mate is the crossroads point. He could either reject this new person and her ideas, or he could act on them. This is a truism for everyone. We will always meet our soul-mate and the meeting will be "set up" by the guide. It can be strangers meeting at a party or can be any social or work encounter. If soul-mates are family members, then there is no meeting necessary.

In the film, the linking of synchronicity with a crossroads point is illustrated by Neo meeting the third central character known as Morpheus. Neo is given one last chance to change his mind, when Morpheus symbolically offers him a blue pill and a red pill with the advice that by taking the red pill *"you stay in wonderland and I show you how deep the rabbit hole goes".* It proved to go very deep, as the rest of the film demonstrated! The scriptwriters' reference to the Lewis Carrol novel neatly drew our attention to synchronicity linked with finding a destiny. This presented itself in the film as two crossroads or decision situations, one the meeting of Trinity and the second the meeting of Morpheus. This is where freewill comes into play. It is our ability to choose between alternatives, one being correct for the life-plan, the other a deviation or delay.

MEETING ONE'S SOUL-MATE

In real life, the synchronicity may be more complex and subtle than the illustration in the film. I will use an example from my own life, that of how I came to meet my soul-mate Angela. In January 2000, a relationship had come to a close and I was seeking a new one. One of the things I did was join an up-market introductions agency. They did an initial screening and fact finding interview. I sent off a large cheque.

In the meantime, I placed an entry in the local newspaper's "dateline" page. It drew several initial responses. At that time

Angela was living alone. Following a miserable Christmas, she had confessed to a work colleague she would like a male friend for occasional outings. She would never have dreamed of responding to "dateline" type adverts. The work colleague suggested she try them, even pointing out one that looked interesting (mine!). Angela still did nothing and put the paper away in a desk drawer. In the meantime I had twice met one of the ladies who had responded to my advert. The work friend again suggested she try the ads. Angela, thinking nothing would come of it as the ad was now some weeks out of date, retrieved the newspaper and rang my advert. She did not know me personally, but being a small town, knew the name when I answered her call. We met for a drink and the rest, as they say, is history. I contacted the introduction agency, who apologised for "mislaying" my application and refunded the fee. How unlike a business organisation to do that, or how like synchronicity. The guide must have been working overtime at this one!

A second illustration is how another couple come to meet. They came to one of my regression workshops, a clue that they are older spirit, as younger spirit would not possess such a degree of enquiry. They lady related how, finding herself divorced and still quite young, she wished to get maximum fun out of being single again. A group of her friends all wished to go to Greece on holiday. As much as she wanted to join them, she felt an urge to go to Mexico on holiday instead, even if that meant going on her own. She was standing by the coffee machine at work and found herself talking to someone she knew only slightly, who also was recently separated and wanted a holiday. She said she could join her going to Mexico if she wished.

She did agree and they both went, the main objective being "to pamper ourselves." One night my regression lady got the urge to go to a particular nightclub. Her friend declined at first to accompany her, but then relented. At that place she met a man younger than herself, but just knew, in the old phrase, he was Mr. Right. The holiday was almost at an end. They only had a morning together before both getting different flights home. She lived in England, he in Seattle, USA.

Back in England, they kept in contact by telephone. Sometimes, she would call him, and he would have already picked up the phone before it rang. My lady subject had a successful career, house and a luxury car, but gave those all up to go and live in Seattle, "just like a student." Of course her friends did not understand her abandoning career and lifestyle, but she was happy. They married and both now live in England.

One can see here classic life-plan synchronicity. The amazing coincidences for the two to meet were spirit-arranged, including her two overwhelming urges, one to go to Mexico, and the other to go out that night to that place. One can also see the spiritual test – does love ignore the opinions of others and take priority over possessions? Her friends said she was foolhardy to make such a dramatic change to her life on the basis of an extremely brief courtship. Of course, not all critical partner meetings need be this convoluted. For some, meeting at college or a workplace is all that is planned. A lot depends on one's spiritual age in how complex the web is weaved.

SUMMARY

We only know if synchronicity is a pointer to destiny, if it is the meaningful type, with hindsight, by what happens afterwards. The other types of synchronicity we might term "everyday angels". There will be many times our guide pulls strings in our life that we do not notice. Thus a phone call can be guide-prompted but we have no awareness it was so arranged unless we spot the happy coincidence of it. For example, we may have just had a customer cancellation that disappoints us and a new enquiry comes along to replace it, seemingly out of the blue, from someone we have not dealt with previously. The coincidence would most likely not be thought of as synchronicity, but in fact, probably was. My guide advises that apart from what he terms acts of daily living, what to eat, what to wear and so on, everything is spirit orchestrated, subject to our freewill choice.

Who would have believed, including myself, that explaining one line of Shakespeare's work would take so much doing. There is much more one could write about the divinity in our lives, but space does not permit. Frank Joseph recommends the keeping of a synchronicity diary. He personally discovered around eight instances per month, or around one hundred per year. For those new to the phenomenon, it is indeed a revelation to spot them in one's own life. It is comforting also to have personal evidence that our lives are predetermined. The big task is in understanding why synchronicity occurs. Frank Joseph recommends meditation to uncover its purpose. That is the best way to develop communication with one's guide. For those like myself who are not self-disciplined enough, a dowsing pendulum is a quick and easy way of receiving an answer, provided one frames the question precisely and provided the guide is willing to answer. After all, he or she does not want to take the fun away by preventing us from making our own "mistakes", which we are here to do as well. If we have the answer paper before we sit the exam, where is the achievement in taking it?

From looking at a source of clues to the planned nature of our individual lives, I now look at the clues to the planned nature of global events. This is not so much the synchronicity of them, but their purpose. In the years preceding 2012, there is much that will happen globally, both human and natural disaster. These are not random events but part of a greater plan.

CHAPTER FIVE

THE POINT OF CHANGE

World events are heading to a crisis point. This point will be one at which, globally, the population wants an end to things the way they are. They will not necessarily know what they want in place, but just that they do not want things to continue in the established pattern. This is the "Point of Change", a most important point in the evolution of the planet. This chapter is devoted to explaining this. It includes new information from the spirit dimension and so will not necessarily therefore have an instant familiarity or have support from other writers to date. New information is given to us as we are considered ready to receive it and the time is correct. The task of introducing new information is usually given to a single, older spirit, as the history of our science demonstrates.

There are an increasing number of people now receiving confirmation from spirit that it is due to occur. There are others that believe the planet is heading to a point of crisis, that there must be change. This is one of the reasons for the shift towards the search for something more, the increased interest in "New Age" pursuits and so on. Some have the unidentified feeling while others have it as a clear thought.

An illustration of this is a question we received from a lady who, in meditation, was presented with a piece of beautiful blue Welsh slate. It just came to her. It then shattered into many pieces and she experienced a frightening feeling. The explanation given by spirit was that this was a symbolic meditation. She was witnessing what has occurred on Earth, represented by the piece of beautiful slate. Spirit created a beautiful planet to give to man. Man has splintered it in so many ways, creating divisions of country, race, colour or creed. He has created borders and boundaries, both physical and mental and in doing so has shattered the unity of the planet. People once citizens of Earth are no longer so. The fright that was felt was the unsettling feeling of inner knowing that the point of final shattering is close and this will be more than has been experienced so far.

Those that practice, or have benefited from, spiritual healing, may know it is not unusual for the patient to go through a "healing crisis". That is, the symptoms will get worse before they get better. So it is with the planet. In certain sectors of certain populations, there will be an increase in the baser side of human instinct in order to get to this point of change. There will be more crime, more unrest, more violence and so on, until those that do not form part of that sector, the majority, cry enough! There will be a point at which many refuse to live in the world with the pain and suffering created by these minority factions, and will seek to change matters.

Governments which do not address the problem will fall; those that appear to do so while doing nothing will fall. In time, spirit advises me, we will have "in power" those who will be genuine in their care for the people of the planet, rather than for themselves. How we govern ourselves will be very different from how it is now, so "in power" will not mean what it does now.

The Point of Change has many opportunities written into the plan for the planet for it to occur. This is because if it is missed at the first opportunity, others are available. It may be within the lifetimes of the current population, but if it occurs on the last attempt, this is two generations away. Spirit assures me if it takes to the last attempt, then plans are in place to make certain it happens then. There has been much comment on the significance of the year 2012. The ancient Mayan civilisation had great astronomy skills. They studied the movement of celestial bodies and could predict accurately future changes in alignments, for example, the times of solar and lunar eclipses. They saw such major alignment changes happening on 21 December 2012, they interpreted them as the end of the world. In fact what they foresaw was the first opportunity for the planet's vibration to change. It will take some time, depending on the state of the planet, from weeks to years.

I have learned that with spirit, little is simple, so what are the circumstances for the change to be successful in human terms? In my dialogue with spirit, the following have been identified:

1   The majority of the population rejecting violence and a mass prayer or wish for peace.

2   A greater acceptance (in the West at least) of the fact that we reincarnate.

3   The increased use of visualisation, particularly in healing.

4   A certain percentage of the people coming to recognise certain spiritual truths, such as the reason for incarnation.

5   A certain percentage will need to accept the existence of the aura and the role it plays, and the existence of universal energies too.

6   One of the big steps is a beginning within people to view themselves as citizens of Earth, which in turn, leads to them recognising their spiritual relationships to be at least as important as their biological ones.

Realising that relationships with the guide and members of the soul group are more important than biological family relationships will come much later. There are many old spirit now incarnating on the planet to help achieve the change to the new level. These have been termed "Indigo" and "Crystal" children. Some have been here some years; a "wave" arrived in 1997 and 2003, who have yet to reach adulthood. The world needs a certain "critical mass" of enlightened spirit in order to change. All these spirits bring with them their spiritual wisdom. What we are as yet unable to do is to recognise that biological age has no relationship to spiritual age. This will change in the distant future, but will not be in place for 2012. The purpose of the James Twyman "messages from the psychic children", for those familiar with them, is to accustom man to receiving words of wisdom from children, rather than the particular messages they bring.

Concerning the evolution of the planet, where are we now and where are we going? Earth is currently at stage three (or level one), and it is planned it will elevate to stage four (or level two) early in the current two thousand year cycle, which began with the year 2000. To move on from stage three, it is necessary for the population to raise its vibration, which is achieved by an increase in awareness of spirit, which I described earlier. There is a connection between the spiritual level of a planet and its human or human-equivalent population in that the vibrations of both are interconnected and both can only move forward in tandem. The strength and composition of the planet's energy grid is improved by the input of new cosmic energies. The population will have new and altered chakras to deal with this shift to the new level.

The general state that a planet needs to achieve in order to begin the elevation now required is for its populace to be one, to truly be brethren. While our planet has divisions of country, race, religion and so on, this cannot be. In higher evolved worlds, one is a child of the planet (or even the universe, or even not of that restriction). One accepts the beliefs of the planet, not of this or that country, or this or that religion. In addition, for a planet to be able to advance, it requires the populace to harmonise with the planet, rather than to rape it.

The reason the world's population is at a peak at the moment is so that more spirit can experience the coming change of vibration in the planet. The population is high so that many can take part in the variety of experiences provided to date and in the experiences to come as the crisis is reached, to assist in the reaching of the crisis and to experience the change, the move forward.

I would now like to quote verbatim, information received from spirit, that is from my guide, who is an old spirit who speaks with the approval of Spirit Council, the body of spirit responsible for carrying out the wishes of the Collective in the evolution of all planets.

"It is necessary for man to raise his spiritual vibration in order for the planet to take the next step in its evolution; in order for it to

raise to the second level and no longer be a nursery world. The whole of man's history to date has been working towards this. In the nursery level, it is correct for a race to experience and to <u>work through</u> its lessons taught by warlike behaviour and negative emotions, its bigotry, its dependence on religion and doctrine; to quickly reach an understanding that peace and harmony is the preferred state.

"I will just reiterate at this point, that in all races beginning at the level of nursery world, which of course, all races have done over the eons, the progress of their development works in the same way; that is that the race works through all the negative aspects, until globally they realise that, to put it simply 'this is not the way, there must be a better way than this', and they then globally raise their awareness, lifting themselves and their world to the next level.

"This is always the case, the only difference is time taken in the achievement. In the case of man, the blueprint used for the species has allowed this to take longer. In man we [Spirit Council] created a species that has continued in the negative, without realising that the change to the utopia they glimpse as provided by the positive, is in their own hands; a species that allows a few to speak for the many and so absolves itself of responsibility in this way; a species that happily assumes the role of victim rather than rise up and change matters. Again, before you leap to the defence, this is as intended for the great wealth of experience it provides. In Earth we intended to provide much experience for many, while the planet retained its nursery status, and this we have done.

"Now, it is time for the planet to enter its next phase, to accelerate towards the point of growth, to be ready when the time is right for its departure from nursery world status. There is a time for this within the greater plan and events will now be engineered to make sure all arrives on cue.

"This is all as intended, the new wave of experiences to come, after a period in which your planet has experienced, by its standards, a degree of settled contentment, at least in certain countries, will lead to the global understanding of a need for change. A recognition that the 'peace and contentment' was only illusory and only *experienced by a comparatively small percentage of the populace at the expense of the greater percentage and was therefore not peace and contentment at all globally.*

"There will be events caused by religious fanaticism, by indigenous disaster and by misplaced 'policing', until the point is reached when it is understood that the power and the decision process should be in the hands of the many and not the few. That decision for the way of life of the majority cannot be handed to a few so that the many may rid itself of responsibility for the outcome. I could go further here, but I believe you both understand the eventual goal striven for in order for the planet to progress.

"During all of this, the imbalance in the earth energies (i.e. universal energies) will play its part, and as they 'gradually' settle, both naturally and by the ministrations of those that are intended to minister to them, they will have an effect on the populace, helping to bring about the understanding and the need for change that will in the first instance, create many of the experiences to come. They are providing a healing catalyst, a healing crisis for the planet, in the same way that many forms of healing in the person cause a healing crisis before true improvement can be experienced. The difference here is that this healing crisis will take years rather than weeks."

Those that have known there was much more than met the eye to the tragedy of September 11th 2001, and the subsequent "War on Terror", will now appreciate that this was the start of the healing crisis. The Enron financial disaster in the USA delivered the same spiritual message as the Twin Towers. These were spiritually intended events designed to affect our thinking. They are planned "wake-up calls", to move man forward to the realisation that must be reached, so the planet can progress. Not so much pride before a fall, but a re-education, a means of teaching what is important, what should be pursued and what should not! It is no accident that the USA has reached the power and wealth that it has. This is a spiritual intention so that it may serve as the tool of tuition for others. What marked out the war on Iraq from all previous wars was the numbers of people who came out in protest against it, knowing it was not the way. Thus it slowly begins; the change in our consciousness necessary to bring us to the Point of Change. Once that is reached, the Way of Change will be seen and then established. For the planet to now move onward, it must move backwards, backwards to its true spiritual nature.

THE SPIRITUAL SIGNIFICANCES OF 9/11

In order for the changes to take place, the population must see the error of its ways. Sometimes "seeing the light" only takes place after a series of disasters and repeated suffering. Man can be quite stubborn in refusing to change his thinking. This is where the events of 9/11 and others of similar purpose come into the plan. The events of that dreadful day go deeper than the visual aspect of a group of fanatical terrorists causing massive loss of life, destruction and suffering. These terrorists would be acting out their own life-plans in perpetrating this deed and in so doing, would undoubtedly set in motion changes within the world. These changes may well be for the worse before they are for the better, but changes for the better will eventually be made as a direct consequence of that day.

Although comparatively few will see it in these terms, the message being delivered is that the West has gone too far down the material road and needs to find the spiritual path once more. We now have the opportunity to use this disaster for good. Rather than seek "justice" at all costs and return an eye for an eye and a tooth for a tooth, should not the question be asked, "What brought the tragedy about?" Why does a group of people in one country hate the culture and all that another stands for to such a degree that they could carry out such an atrocity? What steps could be taken by both sides towards mutual understanding and acceptance? It is understandable that in their pain, some of the bereaved may have wished vengeance, but what does vengeance achieve? Having killed those who killed our own, are we then to carry on as before, having achieved only a widening of the gulf between peoples? (Look at the example of the Middle East conflict).

Spiritual truths are very often given to us as paradoxes. We should not take events for what they seem at first sight, but look for deeper meaning. There are a host of lessons to be seen in the events of 9/11 and I list a few of them:

> The motivational power of belief in reward in an **afterlife**. In the West we are almost defenceless against the suicide bomber. Most are in denial about the very concept of an afterlife, let alone question whether the terrorists are correct in their interpretation. If we had widespread recognition of a major spiritual truth, that we are all on a journey of experiences that features reincarnation into many different and varied cultures, we would look upon our fellow man quite differently.

> It is our **beliefs that determine behaviour**. It follows therefore that if we wish to change behaviours, we must change the way people think. Increasing the defence budget will not achieve this, which was the knee-jerk reaction in the USA. Belief systems in their own history that begot and then fuelled warfare are the War of Independence and the Civil War. It was one of the War of Independence philosophers, Tom Paine, who observed, "*You cannot conquer an idea with an army*".

> The **futility** of hugely expensive and complex weapons systems when set against surprise and simplicity. There never can be ultimate security, even if "Star Wars" technology is put in place. Only when it is realised that we are one human race and one planet, can true peace come about. We do not realise that the divisions we create are those created by our thoughts, and are not true differences at all.

> The **excess of capitalism** as symbolised in the World Trade Centre inspires animosity when the wealth of one nation is not used to benefit others but only itself, and even then only a minority of its population. Perhaps we need a system of exchange that does not involve exploitation of man by fellow man; that does not allow huge wealth to be accumulated by a tiny number of individuals and countries whilst the majority live in poverty.

> The **fragility of the economic system** of the West. It is so poorly founded that in the scale of things, one disaster such as this can affect dramatically the whole economy. It

is not built on solid foundations of honesty and fair dealing but on greed and excess.

➤ We humans are **fear-based in our actions** – the subsequent collapse in air travel, for example. Biological weapons used on the smallest scale, cause huge disruption and terror. If we tried to be love based, what an uplift would be seen in our lives. Love is the true means of dealing with enemies and bringing harmony to the world.

➤ For the cost of all the bombs and missiles used in seeking out the extremists in Afghanistan, the whole country could have been rebuilt. An opportunity was missed to show, **rather than a vengeful USA, a munificent one**.

If you were personally affected by the events of 9/11 or lost one close to you in the disaster, it is our hope that this analysis may give some solace to you. Those that died did not do so in vain, but did so that the world may go forward in the fullness of time, into a new era of mutual understanding and peace.

Although as a race we still have some way to go, it is encouraging to see that there were numerous voices raised against war; even among the bereaved there were calls for peace from those enlightened souls who could see that this was a time for a change in reactions. Numerous groups began world prayers for peace and similar activities, so it begins! Slowly, slowly, but maybe, just maybe the reason for 9/11 will begin to be understood by greater numbers and the world can lift its vibration by raising its spiritual awareness. Following the 3/11 bombings in Madrid in 2004, what was hugely encouraging was the spontaneous protest by millions in Spain against the outrages.

THE SPIRITUAL SIGNIFICANCES OF WAR IN IRAQ

The major players in the conflict, Bush, Blair, Hussein and so on, are carrying out their individual life-plans in doing what they have done to create the situation. These individual life-plans are threads woven on a greater tapestry that is the plan for the planet itself, a plan that is written in periods of two thousand years. The last one ended in the year 2000 and we are now in the new cycle. What is intended in the current cycle is that man climbs up spiritually, by realising the error of his ways.

We have been sent teachers in the past who have led by example and given us a message by which to live. One such was Gandhi. The famous American general, Douglas MacArthur said about him, *"In the evolution of civilisation, if it is to survive, all men cannot fail eventually to adopt Gandhi's belief that the process of mass application of force to resolve contentious issues is fundamentally not only wrong but contains within itself the germs of self-destruction".* How much the present leaders in America have forgotten that and so must relearn it by the war in Iraq and other events. In chapter eight I look at the differing attitudes to the 9/11 tragedy, and attempt to relate them to spiritual age.

Just as an individual can be said to attract the illness that he or she needs for the spiritual growth that can arise from it, so that war in Iraq is an experience on a global scale for its potential to prompt growth. The lessons it provides include the following:

> ➢ The discrediting of existing institutions (UN, NATO, European Alliance, Arab League) as being impotent because of division, and powerless to deal with the problem of a dictator. This situation shows the need for a true world government capable of affecting the will of the majority on a delinquent state.

> ➢ The hypocrisy of the world's superpower in being the principal manufacturer, exporter and holder of weapons, who expects a smaller state to whom it once sold weapons, to disarm. What is required is for an example to be set by the bigger states in giving up their own so-called "weapons of mass destruction"; this might lead the way for them to be discarded by all nations.

> ➢ At a time when one billion people live on less that a dollar a day, the USA has spent seventy five billion dollars on a war, brought about by its own fears. Resentment against the American wealth by the world's poor would be lessened if it spent similar sums on helping others.

> All world history has shown that violence often begets violence and that in doing what it has, the USA is creating a greater long term problem in feeding the motive for future acts of terrorism. The war will not alter terrorists' thinking for the better, nor lessen their grievances.

> As with all previous wars, a tiny number of people have taken decisions that affect many, even when a substantial number have voiced their objection. Our democracies function in name only. We are disempowered as individuals and need to question how better we might take collective decisions.

> The fact that Iraq has the second largest reserves of oil is an unspoken factor in the war. It is interesting that there has been a call by some for the country's oil to be under UN control "in trust for the people of Iraq". As oil was formed millions of years ago by the action of sunlight before man evolved, can it be said to belong to those who happen to live on the surface over its presence? Should not the call be extended and consider the oil as indeed all natural resources, as belonging to both no one and everyone and it be held in trust for the whole of mankind?

There are other lessons too, but the main one is the need to discard violence as the only response to violence; for the majority to see the futility of it and bring into question "Wild West" thinking so having an elevated response and attitude. The planet cannot move forward until the enlightened minority view has been turned into the prevailing attitude of a majority. It is ironic the Americans have (or had) on their currency the Latin tag "e pluribus unum" (out of many comes one), appropriate because of their history of diverse immigration. Apply that to the world, and we have the thinking for global peace.

My quoting Gandhi prompts me to say how all his work is undone in not just the partition of India, but massively so, in both India and Pakistan holding nuclear weapons, and their coming to war and squabbling over who governs Kashmir. The October 2005 earthquake there with 54,000 killed and 2 million homeless are the statistics of a nuclear explosion. One of several lessons here is for the government and people to realise the folly on spending money on weapons and militarising Kashmir when this disaster shows the government lacks the resources to look after its own people in a high risk earthquake zone, and fails to plan adequately for such eventuality. What distorted priorities in lands of poverty. The Western response with aid has been pitiful. We are far from recognising humanity is all one. Will it take a global threat of an asteroid before we do come together?

World events are not only pre-planned but have teaching purposes behind them. We are normally too preoccupied to see the lesson. I would now like to examine one such event in detail, the sinking of the *"Titanic"*, to show how it was spiritually arranged and why. I also use it to illustrate why our opinions can vary so much about the same event, which is differing spiritual ages.

CHAPTER SIX

TITANIC REVISITED

"Titanic" is almost the ship that never sank – there have been so many books and films about the renowned sinking on her maiden voyage, the ship lives on in the public imagination, more so than any other vessel in history. Is there a spiritual reason for that and is there a spiritual perspective to the drama of its brief life? Yes to both! It was spiritually intended that the ship does not fade from consciousness. There are many lessons for Western man to see, if he has eyes to see them. This chapter is an attempt to explain the *"Titanic"* disaster from a completely different viewpoint from the historians, an explanation from the spiritual perspective.

There is no such thing as an accident in spiritual terms. By that I mean, a major disaster, whether manmade, as in this instance, or natural, as in a major earthquake, for example, is known in advance in the spirit dimension. This is because the future is written or planned before it happens. We are the human actors that bring to life those events on the stage of the physical world. Similarly, each human life has a plan composed for it before incarnation. In arriving at that plan, a spirit may or may not take into account and incorporate in some way, events that are known are going to take place. If so, the timing of the incarnation will be such so as to be able to participate and so gain the required experience from the life. On Earth, spirit of the variety capable of incarnating as human, uses the physical body to acquire experiences of that which I call "unconditional love", in the absence of a more accurate description. As spirit we all know what that is; the point of incarnation is to have practical, hands-on, "got the tee shirt" experience of it. I give a complete list of the syllabus in chapter nine.

Many of the participants in the *"Titanic"* disaster and those affected indirectly by it, will have known in the spirit dimension in advance of incarnation that it was destined to happen. Indeed, the twenty-four hour period of 14th and 15th April 1912, the night of the sinking, may have been the major reason for the life, to participate in the event. For those that survived the remainder of their lives would have been affected in some profound way. Whilst those that perished returned to the spirit dimension, the families and those close, would experience for some time the emotions surrounding the loss of loved ones. In human terms, the loss of so many lives was indeed tragic. From the spiritual perspective, the participants will have obtained growth and increased their knowledge of unconditional love in some way.

As with any event involving large scale sudden death, the many acts of cowardice and bravery, of selfishness and unselfishness, or emotion generated through causing death, and witnessing it, and so on, were what the *"Titanic"* tragedy created an opportunity to experience. If spiritual growth were not achieved in the lifetime from these experiences, it would be in the life-review all spirit go through after physical life is over. The tragedy of the *"Titanic"* has a spiritual explanation on both the individual level and on that of the wider Western world. I will look first at the bigger picture and then at some more of the reasoning for the individuals who took part.

The disaster needs to be seen in the context of the changes that were happening in Western society, the social, political and economic background. On the political scene, the European powers were moving towards war. There was, amongst other developments, an arms race taking place. For Britain and Germany, this involved the building of monster warships known as Dreadnoughts. This had begun in 1906 when Britain launched the first of this new type of battleship. Its ten, twelve-inch calibre guns made all other ships obsolete at a stroke. Other nations, too, scrambled to not be left behind in the prestige and security these ships were perceived to bestow. France, Russia, Italy, Japan and the United States had been building up their naval strength besides Britain and Germany. Dreadnoughts were the "must have" defence weapon, essential for any state that saw itself as a maritime power.

In the commercial world, competition had caused the size of passenger ships to increase to Dreadnought proportions. This was particularly so for the North Atlantic passenger trade and particularly the rivalry between the shipping lines of Germany, Britain and the USA. The latest twists in this rivalry had been the British company Cunard launching the then largest ships afloat, *"Lusitania"* and *"Mauretania"* in 1907. The American-owned White Star Line counter-attacked with the order in 1908, for two ships fifty percent larger, *"Olympic"* and *"Titanic"*. The Germans in 1912 launched an even bigger ship than the *"Titanic"*, the *"Imperator"*.

The First World War was an intended event spiritually. When the planetary plan was written, just as is the case for individual plans also, opportunities were incorporated in the plan where through free-will choice, a deviation or alternative path could be taken. This is where the *"Titanic"* tragedy has an explanation. The loss on the maiden voyage of the world's largest ship naturally sent a shock-wave through civil society. It was also an opportunity for reflection for those politicians and military leaders responsible for the naval arms race that was going on to reconsider their thinking. Because of their armour plating, watertight compartments and so on, Dreadnought type ships were considered by their designers and builders to be "unsinkable". Here was a ship, a commercial vessel admittedly, but one similarly trumpeted as "unsinkable", doing exactly what is was not supposed to do.

The sinking presented a chance to reconsider whether the vast expenditure on battleships was the most appropriate one and whether the naval rivalry would have as tragic an outcome as the passenger ship one had. (In the event, the ships were not a decisive weapon. The Battle of Jutland in 1916 was inconclusive, and the big ships spent most of the war in harbour). The naval race was one factor why World War One happened. Its removal would not necessarily have prevented it, but a warning light concerning misplaced confidence in "unsinkable" warships was shone. Few, if any, noticed it. Whether an accident is spiritually intended or not is usually seen by what happened afterwards. If there had been no loss of life resulting from *"Titanic's"* collision, then that would be an indicator it was unintended. With 1,502 lives lost it was the worst maritime disaster in history. The First World War was a little over two years away, in which fifteen million would lose their lives. National shipping lines competed for the biggest ship. Western nations were in competition for the size of their Empires and navies. They also strove to preserve or raise their respective world position in trade and prestige. So, too, did the shipping lines.

A ship, to some extent, is a microcosm of the civilisation that builds it. The technology embodied in its design and construction and its apparatus will reflect the state of knowledge of the society. In the case of passenger ships, the class structure of the civilisation may be visible in the design and internal comforts. The ethos and values of a society may be reflected. The *"Titanic"* was built to appeal to the vanity of the rich, to give them a floating hotel that sped across the Atlantic. It was also a symbol of what the Victorians termed "progress", the advance of human skill and genius in making things and moulding the environment. Thus two more spiritual purposes can be seen in the brief life of the ship – a warning against complete faith placed in "progress" and the inequality of treatment of one human by another when as tragic simultaneous death shows, we are all equal in our fate, whether millionaire or pauper.

Contrary to belief in some quarters, the *"Titanic"* was not, in fact, a technological marvel. Where it broke new ground was in its splendours – the first ever swimming pool on board a ship, a gymnasium, a Turkish bath and a squash court, a mini-hospital, a photo development room, an à la carte restaurant open all hours. (Ironically, had the design followed Brunel's innovation two generations earlier, of a complete double hull, the boat would have probably survived the glancing impact with the iceberg.) It was the biggest and most luxurious ship ever built, the largest moveable manmade object.

As such, it was eminently suitable to serve as a reminder that what human ingenuity can achieve can also fail; that if man allows himself to feel master of his universe the memory of *"Titanic's"* fate may serve to bring him back to a more realistic view of himself. Just as it is sometimes an individual's challenge chosen for the life to keep ego in balance, not to allow oneself to be insufferably vain, nor to be immobilised through a lack of self-esteem, so it is with nations. The Western world at that time had become so mesmerised with its capabilities, it was out of balance (and remains so). Similarly, a spiritual reason for the British fatal charge of the Light Brigade in the Crimea in 1854 can be seen. It was intended as the blow to national pride that it was, the British ego having become inflated, hubris mounted following the Great Exhibition of 1851. The Twin Towers disaster of 11th September 2001 is not dissimilar here in one of its purposes. The West has gone too far down the road of overblown self-belief, at the expense of its spirituality.

That lack of spirituality is seen also in the Edwardian class system that the *"Titanic"* mirrored. In the spirit dimension all spirit, billions of them, are equal. They just vary in the amount of experiences they have had. On Earth, race, class and money are the basis for huge inequalities. The British and Americans, known as the "Anglo-Saxons" at the time, saw themselves as superior to all others. There was racial, class and gender discrimination in who survived and who perished. Sixty-three percent of first class passengers survived but only twenty-five percent of third class. Seventy-four percent of women passengers were saved but only twenty percent of the men. Many of the third class passengers were Irish. The sixty or so Italian staff who manned the à la carte restaurant were confined below decks and none survived. Particularly in the USA, the tragedy gave rise to much debate about class, gender and race. One of the spiritual aims was to prompt discussion about these topics and this it did.

The disaster produced some heroes and villains in the press subsequently. This was an intended consequence spiritually. One of the many facets of "unconditional love" is admiration. Hero-worship is a sort of love at a distance, providing the opportunity for admiration, approval and pride in one's fellow man or woman. There were heroes amongst the crew, which entered into popular narrative. Reverential sentiments were typified by those on the headstone of Ernest Freeman, *"Titanic's"* chief steward. *"He Remained at his Post of Duty, Seeking to Save Others, Regardless of his Own Life, and Went Down with the Ship"*. Perhaps the most popularised was the actions of the senior radio operator, Jack Phillips. He remained at his post even after released from duty by his captain, desperately trying to find another ship closer to the *"Titanic's"* position than the *"Carpathia"*. In the United States, Molly Brown became a heroine of epic proportions. Her efforts to assist needy survivors financially continued for twenty years. The legend of the "Unsinkable Molly Brown" began after her death with two fictionalised books in the 1930s and then continued in a musical and film in the 1960s.

The sceptic might well ask, how I can possibly assert the *"Titanic's"* sinking was a spiritually intended event without evidence. The actual mechanics of it, as with all life's events, is the actions of spirit guides getting their incarnated counterparts in the right place at the right time. Guides communicate with each other to help bring this about. For anyone whose life is destined to impact on many others, not only will his or her guide at times be present, but others charged with overseeing that life will be also, to give stronger communication with the incarnated spirit. Communication can include actual thoughts, gut feelings, and what I have termed "involuntary urges", the sudden impulse to a course of action without premeditation. The opposite of this which sometimes occurs, is failing to appreciate consequences, having our eye intentionally taken off the ball, so something happens we might otherwise have prevented. We are not consciously aware normally of this communication from our guides which can take these various guises.

We can see spirit at work from what has been termed "synchronicity". That is, an instance of meaningful coincidence, an unlikely combination of circumstances often giving rise to something fairly inconsequential, but later leading on to something far more significant for the person. I set out in appendix one some of the synchronicities regarding the *"Titanic"* disaster. Synchronicities are often only revealed with hindsight. They are the disguised signposts arranged by spirit guides, that point out a destiny, or are evidence of those guides having been at work to facilitate a destiny, as I list here in *"Titanic's"* case.

Other indirect clues to the predestined nature of the tragedy are those passengers and crew that had a premonition or strong sense of foreboding about the voyage. For several people, this was forceful enough to make them leave the ship. Again, this would be their guide at work. With accidents, it is possible to be in the wrong place at the wrong time, and be unintentionally caught up in someone else's fate. Alternatively, having had a "narrow escape" could have been intended for the emotional experiences arising. In total, over fifty people decided not to sail on the maiden voyage and cancelled bookings, including the owner of White Star's parent company, John Pierpont Morgan. To not catch (or leave) a means of transport that has a disaster ending, can be just as much a planned event as catching it.

Only a relatively few people, I suspect, will accept my contention the *"Titanic's"* sinking was pre-planned in the spirit dimension. This leads me to say that Earth is composed of spirit of varying ages, the majority being young spirit, or what I term, level one. (The spiritual journey consists of five levels). There is often a different reaction in people to the same event or circumstances. My explanation for this is that it is because we have different ages spiritually, as well as biologically. Old and young spirit will quite often react in opposite ways to the same experience. Where one sees misfortune, the other might see an opportunity to learn for example. I have in appendix two, set out a number of possible attitudes to the tragedy and alongside each, suggested the likely spiritual age of the person with that opinion. Those that I have described as "spiritually aware" are a minority at present.

The *"Titanic"* disaster has been kept alive in books and films for a spiritual purpose. The teachings it is possible to see in the tragedy are still relevant in today's world. James Cameron's blockbuster 1997 film *"Titanic"* was seen by millions, eighteen million cinema seats being sold in the UK alone. Being Hollywood, the main attention was taken up by the romantic story line, with the ship as the setting. (That did give a spiritual bonus message, however, in portraying that love can transcend physical death.) In a world that continues to be characterised, particularly in the USA, with extremes of wealth for a tiny minority, it is instructive to be reminded in the film that "death levels all". In the final analysis, money and luxury are useless. The questions raised at the time over gender, class and race discrimination still have relevance. We have not yet learned to fully treat all as equal to one another.

The world will not become a better place until we have recognised our spirituality and live less selfishly. Is it a coincidence the centenary of the sinking, 2012, coincides with the year of the first opportunity for the planet to raise its vibration, for there to be an upward shift in human consciousness? It is a feature of human nature that it takes painful experiences usually to alter our thinking. Just as for individuals, so too for nations. The Chernobyl nuclear "accident" was a big stimulus, for example, to change Cold War attitudes in Russia. Let us hope the disasters currently taking place in the world will quickly lead to the lessons they are designed to teach being taken on board by those in positions of responsibility.

To summarise, the spiritual reasoning behind the sinking of the *"Titanic"* was:

- To create a shock for Western man to realise that he is not all-powerful.
- To provide a warning about commercial and economic rivalries having the potential for great disaster.
- To prompt the questioning of race and class and gender discrimination.
- To demonstrate the futility of worshipping wealth.
- To create some heroes as role models.
- To awaken the European powers from their sleepwalk to war through an arms race involving "unsinkable" warships.

Most manmade disasters will have their lessons to teach. What we are not accustomed to is seeing their design, and behind that, the spiritual reasoning, as with the 9/11 New York tragedy. The year 1912 is a further clue to there being a world plan, the timing of this ship tragedy exactly a century from the Ascension date. Of course, that was not known at the time. A modern spiritual interpretation is the ship might be a metaphor for the planet. Not all on board are going to survive the transition from nursery level to the next one. Some will have elected to go down with the ship.

SYNCHRONICITY AND THE "TITANIC"

1. The designer had originally wanted sixty-four lifeboats.
    Against his better judgement the number was reduced first
    to forty-eight and then to thirty-two and finally to sixteen.
    This was the minimum legal requirement but which was
    only sufficient for one-third of the complement. (The
    regulations concerning safety were set out in 1894 and
    envisaged vessels up to ten thousand tons. They had not
    been updated for the ever-increasing bigger ship tonnages.)

2. *"Titanic"* did not follow the recommended route for
    outbound liners at that time of year, which was the
    "Outward Southern Track". Instead the captain followed
    the "Autumn Southern Track", which was the more direct
    route to New York but it took the liner sixty miles north of
    the safer alternative path.

3. It was good practice to double the lookouts in the presence
    of ice. Thus other ships in the locality, *"Californian"* and
    "Carpathia" had done so, but not the *"Titanic"*. Binoculars
    intended for use by the lookouts were normally kept in a
    special cupboard built into the crow's nest. None were
    available for the lookouts since *"Titanic"* left Southampton,
    despite their requests for them.

4. It had become an established custom on Sundays to have a
    lifeboat drill, in which a picked crew would practice
    uncovering and swinging out a boat. On Sunday 14th April,
    the captain decided to forego the drill and held a religious
    service in the first-class dining saloon. (I hesitate to
    highlight another message in the sinking here, that no
    amount of religious devotion will prevent a destiny
    occurring.) Lack of training and inefficient leadership were
    regarded among the causes for the high percentage lost
    (sixty-eight percent).

5. On the Friday night, *"Titanic's"* wireless broke down. It
    was repaired but the seven hours of downtime created a

backlog of messages passengers paid to send to friends, family and business associates. The novelty of being on the world's largest ship encouraged a more than usual number of such messages. The consequences of the breakdown were twofold. The radio operator, Phillips, became exhausted working long hours to deal with the backlog. On Sunday 14th April, *"Titanic"* received seven ice warnings by radio and one by Morse message. Of the seven, it seems three never made it to the bridge, contrary to the rules that navigational messages have priority. (The wireless problem was traced to a faulty lead running from the transformer to the transmitter. As readers may be familiar themselves, spirit can interfere with electrical apparatus, switching it on or off, for example).

6. One ice warning that did not reach the bridge on a timely basis but which reached the captain was one from the *"S S Baltic"* at 1.42pm on the Sunday afternoon, which Captain Smith handed to J Bruce Ismay, the company's managing director. He then kept it for five-and-a-half hours. It was not until dinner that night that Smith asked for the message back and had it posted on the bridge. Ismay, thus had been made aware that ice lay ahead but did not interfere. He had ultimate responsibility for the ship's safety but remained silent.

7. On the other hand, something unusual happened with the wireless operator aboard the *"Carpathia"* that was fortuitous. The operator had no fixed hours, but usually was not expected to be working after 11pm. It was close to midnight when the operator decided to retire to bed. However, he was having trouble with a knotted shoelace, which delayed him and kept him on air for a few minutes longer than he would otherwise have been. Then, "on a whim", he decided to call up *"Titanic"* and let her operator know Cape Race was trying to contact them. He was astonished to receive a call for help in reply, and rushed this to his captain.

8. There was an inexplicable delay between the lookouts

raising the alarm from the crow's nest and the reaction
from officers on the bridge. Two or three times the lookout
tried to raise the bridge by ringing the bell and trying to
phone. When he did get a response, the lookout was
astonished the bridge took no action at all.

9. There was a response, when First Officer Murdoch saw the
    iceberg for himself, but by then it was too late. The sudden
    turn to port ordered by Murdock coupled with reversing the
    engines caused the glancing blow rather than a head-on
    collision. This action was doubly unfortunate; it made a
    collision more certain and prevented the preferable
    outcome of a head-on impact. The ship had been designed
    to withstand a head-on collision and it has been argued,
    may not have sunk. By reversing both engines, in
    "Titanic's" case, the central turbine shut off, depriving the
    rudder of slipstream. To slow and turn away *"is the surest
    possible way of bringing about a collision"* [Knight's
    Modern Seamanship, 1910 edition]. It would have been
    better to put one engine full astern and kept the other full
    ahead with the wheel hard over to turn in the shortest
    possible distance.

Are these points support for the "unforeseen and unforeseeable"
set of circumstances that were held in some quarters to be the
cause of the disaster? Are some of them "human error", so often
found to be the cause of modern day accidents? Yes, but what lay
behind the human error? There is too much here to be just chance
or coincidence. If the *"Titanic"* were the subject of a coroner's
enquiry, there is enough here to confirm a suspicion of foul play,
not return a verdict of accidental death.

Perhaps the most compelling synchronicity surrounding the
"Titanic", is that the disaster was foretold in a novel by the British
author Morgan Robertson in his 1898 book, *"The Wreck of the
Titan; or Futility"*. Comparison of the novel and the real-life
events fourteen years later is far too much for coincidental
probability. The story is of an ocean liner on her maiden voyage
from England, the largest, most luxurious of her kind, eight
hundred feet long with three propellers, striking an iceberg in the

month of April, too few life boats, panic aboard, the ship deemed "unsinkable" by its makers and great loss of life. He almost got the name right, too, if the detail were not convincing enough alone. What the author was doing was being inspired by his spirit guide to produce this supposed fiction. It served to show us that major happenings are known in advance, that they are not accidents, that we can sometimes receive warnings from spirit but, of course, usually fail to see them because of our lack of awareness and vanity.

DIFFERENT ATTITUDES TO THE DISASTER AND POSSIBLE SPIRITUAL LEVEL OF THOSE HOLDING THEM.

Attitude	Possible Spiritual Age
1. The Captain was to blame – he was the one in charge.	LEVEL ONE – Scapegoat or blame a person or institution
2. The shipping company was the cause, because of the lack of lifeboats to save expense and pursuit of a fast crossing to gain publicity.	LEVEL ONE – Scapegoat or blame a person or institution
3. The failure of British regulations to keep up with the times is largely to blame.	LEVEL ONE – Scapegoat or blame a person or institution
4. An act of a vengeful God on a greedy Protestant nation.	LEVEL TWO – Cause and effect – religious extremism or ideological view
5. A consequence of the vulgar pampering to the demands of the rich for luxury at the expense of the workers	LEVEL TWO – Cause and effect – religious extremism or ideological view

6. A series of misjudgements by the ship's officers culminating in the tragedy. (Going too fast; inadequate precautions to deal with ice; failure to process ice warnings properly).

LEVEL THREE – Thoughtful or rational collectivising blame or absolving from blame

7. Not an act of arrogance or negligence by the officers, but a disaster "unforeseen and unforeseeable". An "Act of God".

LEVEL THREE – Thoughtful or rational, collectivising blame or absolving from blame

8. Shameful class and race discrimination resulted in an inequitable proportion of third class passenger and non Anglo-Saxon deaths. "Women and children first" a debatable policy.

LEVEL FOUR – Moral perspective

9. *"A calamity which might well make the proudest man humble".* (George Bernard Shaw) *"The chastening influence it should have on the self-confidence of mankind".* (Joseph Conrad)

LEVEL FIVE – Spiritual or philosophical view

10. A portent of further disasters through national rivalries in commerce and armaments towards which the western nations were sleep-walking.	HIGH LEVEL FIVE – Spiritually aware.

My matching attitude to spiritual level is speculative and something of a sweeping generalisation. A person may have held several of the possible responses that I have listed. I am suggesting likely spiritual age for a stance taken. The reason there was a spectrum of attitudes to the tragedy (and indeed as there is to any major happening in life) is not primarily one of class, educational attainment or other nurture reason, but one attributable to varying spiritual age. Level One spirit certainly would not seek deeper meaning and do not usually recognise their own personal responsibility. I therefore see them as casting blame on institutions or on individuals but without a great deal of analysis, and unlikely to put themselves in the position of the accused party in order to see both sides.

Level Two spirit would be similar in that regard. They tend to hold dogmatic views, including the more extreme religious beliefs. Level Three spirit are often found in the realm of the professional and artistic. I see them as either recognising responsibility as a complex, not simplistic argument or recognising certain events are beyond human control. By Level Four, spirit stops seeing life in black and white, and starts to challenge orthodox views. Level Five spirit are the philosophers who would tend to seek meaning beyond the surface appearance. Those spiritually aware would know *"nothing happens by accident"* and that there would be purpose behind such a disaster. The "don't knows" or "have no opinion" category, which I have not included, would most likely be younger spirit, particularly if they were not personally affected in any way. In contrast to higher level spirit, they tend not to focus too much on anything outside of their daily routine.

The USA Senate enquiry criticised the actions of the crew and conduct of the shipping line. The Board of Trade British enquiry was a far lengthier and more costly one. It concluded the captain had followed accepted practice in not slowing down and it was this that was faulty, not the captain's judgement. There was no scapegoat. The press in both countries interpreted the sinking along similar lines – the United States press pointing the finger at those it considered responsible; the British press more conservative, reluctant to criticise and seeing the disaster as a combination of circumstances.

NOTES FROM THE AUTHOR

In writing this chapter, I am grateful for the source material in Stephanie Barczewski's book, *"Titanic, A Night Remembered"*, published in 2004 by Hambledon & London. My own connections with the *"Titanic"* are tenuous. The date of sailing of the maiden voyage, 10th April, coincides with my birthday. That is not synchronicity, as I explained in chapter four. There are however more clues in the *"Titanic"* story, to the planned nature of world events when one has knowledge of a less well-known ship tragedy. *"Titanic's"* owners, the American White Star Line, had owned thirty-nine years previously, in 1873, a ship known as the *"Atlantic"*, which sank off Nova Scotia in the worst merchant shipwreck up to that time in which 565 people perished. I was one of the Irish crew members on board amongst that number. (This is one of my past lives discussed in *"Why Come Back Book Two"*.)

There are so many parallels between the *"Atlantic"* tragedy and that of the *"Titanic"*, one could believe that one was a rehearsal for the other! In fact, it is an instance of the same event and surrounding set of circumstances being used a second time in the world plan, although each did not have quite the same spiritual purposes. The similarities were: insufficient lifeboats for the numbers carried; passenger accommodation the most luxurious of any ship; the captain was not present on the bridge at the vital time; "culpable" action in heading at full speed at night in proximity to danger (although visibility was good); the same shipping line was involved and the same sea passage, England to New York; omission of one or more navigational practices that might otherwise have prevented the "accident". The thirty-nine year interval between the two disasters is another clue – the number three and its multiple nine, sometimes feature in the world plan as previously mentioned.

I am aware of the conspiracy theory surrounding the *"Titanic"*, that there was an insurance scam, that there was a swap with her sister ship. Spirit tell me this is an unfounded theory. We have in our regression workshops or through mediumship, confirmed to three people that they drowned in the *"Titanic"* disaster. Two of those three already had a strong draw to the story of the ship. One had previously visited a *"Titanic"* exhibition and "felt a shock" on touching a piece of the wreck, but without understanding why at the time. In her home she has a *"Titanic"* wall mirror, one contained within a lifebuoy. She also has a large wall poster in her hall containing the newspaper front page which related news of the sinking. The mediumship we gave explained her fascination. Additionally she discovered her present spirit guide was her husband from the Edwardian period life, who also went down with the ship. I conducted a meditation through which she saw her guide, whose image matched the description earlier obtained through mediumship. This lady is a good example of how what we collect or use to decorate our home is a clue sometimes to a past life experience, or time period of a past life, or past life occupation.

CHAPTER SEVEN

AUSCHWITZ AND THE SEARCH FOR MEANING

Here is a challenge for the would-be spiritual philosopher: explain the meaning of Auschwitz!

The Holocaust Memorial Day and 60th anniversary of the liberation of the infamous place of industrial genocide has been in the news at the time of writing in 2005. This has prompted me to contemplate the painful memory of the events there of 1942-5. How does one begin to understand it? How does the existence of God relate to this? It was just one of many large-scale cruelty and killing events of the twentieth century. What is this world into which we come, apparently not through choice? One does not need medieval conceptions of Hell to imagine it. It is here on Earth now. Is Hell then here? How does one find meaning in this horror, and indeed the whole of the twentieth century, with its wars and disasters and man's inhumanity to man?

THE SPIRITUAL JOURNEY

The spiritual philosophy I have received is as follows. The spiritual journey for all is in outline already laid out. It consists of hundreds of incarnations, five hundred or more, both as a life-form and as an energy-form. These take place on planets in this universe and in a second physical universe. Planet Earth is just one of seventy-five planets in this universe used by spirit. Spirit along this journey, which will take many thousands of years (one hundred thousand is not exceptional), choose prior to incarnation, what it is they wish to experience; what particular aspects of love in either their positive or negative versions they wish to experience, from the detailed syllabus established by the Creator or Higher Power.

This Creator is an intense concentration of very high frequency energy. It is not a biological life-form, it is not humanoid, it is an energy form, which subdivided itself to create seven dimensions, or lower frequency vibrations. This God-energy constitutes a whole separate third universe in itself. When this energy appears in the two physical universes, it is held inside the stars. All stars and all planets are interlinked by straight lines of this energy, which constitutes the life-force. Where a planet holds biological life, the life-force energy gives life to living things and also makes the planet a living, evolving thing too.

All living things need both this life-force and spirit energy in order to exist. We as human beings are a physical body which temporarily houses our spirit or soul. This consists of creation energy, which needs the universal life-force to replenish and to power it. A human body is one of many vehicles for a spirit to obtain experiences. Why does it wish to have experiences? In simplistic terms, this is explained in *"Tomorrow's God"* by Neale Donald Walsch as follows:

> *"What God chooses to do is to know itself in its own experience. This is God's purpose: to know itself wholly.*
> *God can know itself conceptually easily enough. God merely has to think about itself. Yet for God to experience itself, God has to encounter something that God is not. Only through such an encounter can God experience what God is .... God reasoned that since nothing other than God existed, God would have to create something that appeared to be 'other than God' out of itself. God did this by dividing itself into .... billions of smaller parts – and each of those parts would be something other than the totality of God".*

Each of us is one of those billions of tiny parts. At the moment we exist in a three dimensional physical universe, (many here would add time as a fourth dimension). This is the 'realm of the relative' where we have relative experiences. It is outside of the spiritual universe of God-energy, but is connected with it. Before and after an incarnation we inhabit the spirit universe, our natural home. The two physical universes are holders or containers to have every experience it is possible to have. God is the source, the beginning and end for each, on the spiritual journey. God knows all and is all. We co-create through our experiences; we increase knowledge to know ourselves better and in turn, the Creator knows itself better.

The events we experience in a lifetime will have been pre-planned in our spirit state. We write our script and then incarnate to bring it onto the stage, into the physical world. The big events, wars, famines, genocides and pandemics are not scripted by individual spirits, but a sub-committee of God-energy, known as Spirit Council.

EARTH THE PLANET OF NEGATIVE EMOTIONS

In the particular case of Auschwitz, the world events leading up to it and the events that took place there were all scripted or pre-planned. The rise of fascism, of the Nazi party, the persecution of the Jews, World War Two, and so on, were all scripted. When Karl Marx famously wrote, *"men do make their own history, but not in circumstances of their own choosing"*, he was partially correct. We do choose our own circumstances, hard as that is to accept in human eyes sometimes. In spiritual eyes, we choose events and circumstances that are going to lead to spiritual growth and choose experiences we have not had previously.

Painful life experiences can promote rapid learning and spiritual progress, more so than any other way. As planet Earth went through a time of density, darkness and distorted belief systems, many spirits chose that time for an incarnation. It is not a question of karma, the real spiritual meaning of which has been misunderstood; karma is an act of unselfishness for the growth of others. It is not a question of some divine retribution on the Jewish nation. It is normal for one or more cultures to play the "scapegoat" role on a nursery world, the Jews unfortunately taking that role this time. It is a question of challenge and potential growth through experiences and difficulties overcome.

If we were to choose a planet where we could experience the opposite of love, experience barbarity and cruelty on a massive scale, we would choose Earth. Lives on Earth are the contrast to the highest experiences of love that it is possible to have. There is always one such planet with that role at any one time, but thankfully only one. Not only that, there has never been a planet with that role and with a dominant life-form with so little spirituality as that of homo sapiens. We are the real Darth Vaders of the Universe, the species so bent on exploitation, on its ready willingness to extinguish other life, including members of its own species, on its readiness to commit violence and inflict pain for no other reason than that of disagreeing with a person's beliefs.

THE WORLD PLAN

The timing of so much trauma in the twentieth century is not accidental. Just as some composers make the final movement of their symphony an "allegro con brio", one of intensity, tumultuousness and shattering climax, so the twentieth century will turn out in the history of the planet. It was the finale of planet Earth's time as the "nursery world". This explains the explosion of numbers of spirits here to take part in the "unique" experiences to be obtained here. The seemingly impossible task of comprehending why there is so much large-scale suffering, pain and disaster in the world is answered. These events afford a multitude of spirit the opportunity to advance themselves by experiencing what love is not; by experiencing pain, violence and inhumanity in order to have the contrast to love, joy, bliss and harmony at other times in other places. It is one lifetime of trauma to be seen in the context of many other spiritual lives to be lived. It is one life in a spectrum of lives.

Much has been written to analyse how Hitler came to power and was able to initiate the events he did. In human terms, historians point to the Germans feeling of humiliation over the 1919 peace terms, of the economic crisis of the Depression, of the results of propaganda, Nazi fear and intimidation tactics, of the appeal to nationalism, and to anti-Semitism and so on. These are correct, but another level of explanation exists, that of these events being spiritually intended, and indeed, orchestrated from the spirit dimension for the progress of many.

INDIVIDUAL LIFE-PLANS

When Shakespeare, therefore, has Lady Macbeth command:

"Come you spirits
That do tend on mortal thoughts! Unsex me here,
And fill me from crown to toe top full of direst cruelty"

She also speaks for all those perpetrators of genocide and refers to the spirit orchestration of it, both in the twentieth century and earlier ones.

The whole of man's history is scripted, just as individual lives are scripted. Each human actor on the world's stage has a spirit director who "oversees" the life or who does "tend on mortal thoughts" since our thoughts travel into the spirit dimension. Beyond individual spirit guides, there are others tasked with helping to bring to life the world plan. This all takes place in an invisible, unseen, unfelt manner. An exception is when we spot instances of "synchronicity", that is the occurrence of an incident in a life that is beyond mere statistical probability. It is our evidence of the spirit guides at work.

Before an individual spirit incarnates and takes expression, it knows in broad outline, what is going to happen in the life to come. Indeed, the spirit will have chosen to have certain experiences and these will be the reason for incarnation. The spirit seeks challenges in order to have some experience of the phenomenon I have called "unconditional love". This involves experiencing love from the perspective of what it is not, as well as what it is. So in the case of the 1.1 million tragic Auschwitz deaths, those involved may have experienced one or more of the following, in its most opposite aspect; allowing a frame of reference to be built when added to other lives:

(a) compassion, empathy, kindness and consideration
(b) care, concern and education
(c) tolerance, forbearance and patience
(d) acceptance of difference, faith and belief
(e) peace, harmony, amity and freedom from strife.

No doubt those involved would comment, "You can say that again!" No matter how hideous the death, the spirit or soul would be unaffected in any physical way. It would of course have the memory of the experience. It is true that in the case of violent death, particularly if one was aware of one's fate for a period beforehand, the memory can be etched deeply and the spirit can be traumatised for a period. On return to the spirit dimension, all those from Auschwitz would be met on the other side by their spirit guide, as are all spirit. If they require it, they would have undergone the equivalent of convalescence period. Similarly, prior to incarnation, young spirit would have received guidance and tuition or "trauma counselling" for those who required it.

We have, in our regression workshops, had some participants recall the passing back to the spirit state at the end of their last incarnation. They recall being surrounded by love and had the feeling of "coming home". Tears of joy were shed at this recall; confirmation of their inner knowing that spirit is the natural state and incarnation the unnatural one. It may be worth quoting here the description of the spirit realms given by Silver Birch, the name of the spirit guide to Maurice Barbanell, bringer of philosophy in the 1930s:

"Yet that which you see [on Earth] is but a very, very pale reflection of the beauties that we have in our world of spirit. We have flowers such as you have never seen; we have colours such as your eye has never beheld; we have scenes and forests; we have birds and plants; we have streams and mountains. You have nothing to compare them with. And you will be able to enjoy them. Even though you will be "ghosts", you will be real ones."

The spirit dimension is our natural home, the place we are normally. To be in a biological body is the exception to the norm. We do so in order to have practical experiences, the only way a spirit can achieve progression through the various dimensions in spirit, and so return back to the Source. One cannot evolve spiritually without the hands-on experiences of passing through nature. Thus the whole Nazi phenomenon, including the holocaust, will have advanced many on their spiritual journey. It is true this was by negative experiences, but those are just as vital as the positive ones.

Although there will be no permanent effects for those having suffered at Auschwitz, there can be unintentional consequences in subsequent incarnations. This is particularly so if the next incarnation quite quickly follows on, which in our terms is within a century. What happens is that certain phobias or physical symptoms manifest, which are misplaced because of the temporary amnesia we all suffer on incarnation has not been one hundred percent. The horror of the gas chambers does not come through as an actual memory, but might as an inexplicable fear of showers because of the Germans' misuse of the word, and might as asthma symptoms because of the memory of suffocation. [Bringing such memories into conscious awareness is a large step on removing their consequences, which combined with spiritual healing should remove the problem.] Major depression can sometimes have a past life origin. A prolonged period of extreme stress, such as a concentration camp one, can give rise to "reincarnational depression". This emotional scarring can be healed and removed, once correctly identified.

It would be not only the victims but also the perpetrators who obtained spiritual growth. All spirits will experience violent death on the spiritual journey, some many times. Similarly all spirit will experience times as perpetrators of violence and as witnesses to it. This is all to learn through practical experience the nature of love. Thankfully these lives are a small part of the total number, and are usually experienced by spirit in the early stages of their career.

I have not mentioned "grief" so far, perhaps because it seems so obvious, but which ought not to be omitted. "Grief" in the context of 'unconditional love' is not limited to the experience of the death of a loved one, but is much wider in scope. Grief is the antonym of joy and provides a balance to the lessons joy gives. Grief not associated with death has many guises, not perhaps labelled grief but having a similar quality. This can be caused by loss of status, loss of livelihood, loss of any kind, even anticipated loss. I imagine many of the Jewish community suffered these in the 1930s in Hitler's Germany.

A CASE STUDY

All the participants in the holocaust will have had their own particular spiritual reasons for their experiences. I now look at two such individuals as a case study.

I have written that the encounter with one's soul-mate can be for sorrow as well as joy. He or she can at times bring great distress to one's life, even be the cause of one's demise. We have had a fascinating regression experience of two young ladies at one of our workshops that is an example of this and also of survival of Auschwitz and of fairly rapid reincarnation, at least in spiritual terms. The details are as follows.

In the current life, the two are twin sisters. One of them had a feeling that she had killed her sister in a past life, but did not have precise facts, just a feeling. It can often happen if one dies a violent death, or in this example commits violence, and one reincarnates within a century, one can bring unintentional feelings about that past life into the current one. [In my own example I have always had a draw to the First World War, not understanding why, until I saw the trenches in a regression experience and so learnt I had been there.]

For those not familiar with reincarnation, I remind the reader one is not always the same gender. In the regression, one of the twins saw a concentration camp. She had recently visited Auschwitz and wondered if that was what she was seeing. (Having a draw to a particular place or country is sometimes a clue to a past-life connection.) She saw a soldier first and then a Jewish man and so was confused about which she was. Through mediumship, her guide explained that she was a German soldier who was detailed to the Auschwitz camp and gave her the name in that life. In the camp was one prisoner who played the viola most beautifully. He was entranced by the playing and formed a tentative friendship with the musician. This made it the more difficult when he was called on to assist in the termination of this man. At this point he hated being German, hated being himself, hated his race and what they were doing and ended his life because of what he had to do.

The viola player is her twin sister in the present life! They are soul-mates, hence the confusion about which person she was in the regression images. In the case of the camp guard, the life was chosen as one of contrast to a Native American life when he had pride in her people and their life, pride in their beliefs and their interaction with nature, rather than pride of self. The Auschwitz life was to experience the opposite to the Native American. Pride in one's nationality is demonstrated as much by lack of it as it is by feeling it. One needs to experience both sides of the situation to obtain a full understanding. This is a basic feature of the whole spiritual journey, that of duality or contrast.

Just as this is experienced by individuals, so can a particular emotion be experienced by nations. Up until 1942 no doubt many in Germany felt pride in their military victories and the superiority of their race. When the full horrors of Auschwitz become known, no doubt many felt the shame and revulsion that our regression lady recalled.

A HUMANITY FEATURE

We should not feel the horror of Auschwitz was a German aberration, nor one of that time only. We have a habit of stereotyping ourselves into gender and racial types. All human beings are individual spirits choosing to incarnate. They choose various nationalities and cultures along the journey. What varies is the spiritual age of each and their life plan. We can choose to be German, American, French, Aborigine, Native American or Japanese, any nationality. It is one of having personal preference and wishing to have a variety of experiences in different cultures. One man in his time plays many parts, as Shakespeare said.

One does not need to look far to see it is not particular nations but much of the human race that is capable of barbaric acts. For example, in the English Civil War, a once peaceful nation descended into brutality. Individuals once tied by friendship, marriage and social position, became enemies and inflicted violence upon each other. (Propaganda played an important role for the first time in that war; it was not first discovered by the Nazis.) In World War Two the British policy of carpet-bombing German cities remains controversial, especially the later stages and Dresden in particular. What had the citizens of Dresden done to harm the British? If one looks at the United States, some argue the wiping out of the Native Americans was an act of genocide. The Americans hurried use in 1945 of the atomic bomb killed many innocent Japanese civilians, merely because of their nationality, no vital military target was the excuse. The defeat of the Nazis did not end the human phenomenon of state-sanctioned mass murder. There are later European and Third World examples – Bosnia, the Kurds in Iraq, the Tutsis and Hutus in Rwanda and recently Darfur. A United Nations 1948 convention on genocide did not prevent these events.

INEVITABLE?

An interesting question arises, could Auschwitz have been prevented? It is possible to say it could have been delayed, but only rarely does a major predestined event not occur in the plan for the planet. There are opportunities built into the plan where a choice is presented and an intended event may or may not occur. If it does not, a second or even a third opportunity may be in the plan for it to do so. In the case of World War One, as previously related, the sinking of the *"Titanic"* in 1912 was the opportunity for politicians to pull back from the "sleepwalk" into European War. It needed the insight to see in that tragedy that it was the commercial rivalry of national shipping lines, which exemplified the colonial and trade rivalries of the European powers at the time, that ultimately caused the disaster, and which was an omen or portent. Similarly there was an opportunity built into the world plan for World War Two to be avoided, or rather delayed.

This was in 1936 when Hitler reoccupied the Rhineland. Most historians now recognise this was the opportunity missed by the Western democracies to prevent world war in 1939. Hitler was too weak militarily to risk war with Britain and France at that time. The Western democracies' leaders had pusillanimous and vacillating behaviour. By the time they found the resolve to confront Hitler, it was too late. (This failure has perhaps contributed to an over compensatory effect subsequently in politicians, eager to confront those regarded as the new Hitler, such as Nasser or Hussein.) Had Hitler been resisted in 1936, a second opportunity for World War was in the plan six years later than when it did happen.

Hitler is now infamous for the murder of six million Jews and Slavs. He is, however, but one of the troika of mass murderers of the twentieth century. Estimates vary of the numbers killed in the 1930s in Russia, under Stalin's policies of deliberate famine, forced labour and liquidation, somewhere between nine and twenty million died. In China, Mao's rule produced mass death also. The famine produced by the Great Leap Forward killed twenty to thirty million. The Cultural Revolution killed an unknown number. The appearance yet again of the number three, in three great tyrants following each other, is a clue to the planned nature of world events.

This inhumanity to man is both a hard-wired feature of human behaviour and spiritually intended as an extreme of emotion to be experienced uniquely on a nursery planet. Emotions can be the greatest route to spiritual growth. Even negative ones, such as fear, inner loathing, and so on can actually serve a purpose in this way, just as can joy, love, and other positive emotions.

WHY DID IT HAPPEN?

Academics have commented on some common features of these mass genocides: the complete absence of moral restraint in the leaders; the use of terror to subdue populations; the use of ideology to transform the moral identity of peoples. If one ever needed a demonstration of the power of ideology, here it is in triplicate. The Nazi ideology as we know, spoke of superior and inferior races; the communism of Stalin and Mao required the elimination of people who were said to hold back their "utopian" vision of the people's state. In the greater plan, what fascism and the communism of Stalin and Mao teach us, is that these are not the means to achieve a better way of life for all, how huge distortions of the truth and justice lead to misery and inhumanity. There can be no

Utopian civilisation whilst a corrupt few hold sway over the many. These dictatorships will serve as examples to look back upon how not to organise ourselves as a society, not to allow authority to be in the hands of the few.

In understanding how Auschwitz could have happened one must realise how easily we as human beings give away our independence of thought, and so allow an ideology to take hold in our minds, just as a virus might do in our bodies. To resist propaganda people need the ability to think critically. Some do not have this faculty. Some that do chose not to use it, preferring to be relieved of having to think. We, as a species, do this all the time. It is easier to listen to a so-called expert, self-styled guru, political leaders and so on, rather than arrive at our own opinion. This again will be the contrast to other lives when we do not allow this to happen. When it does happen, it provides a challenge to resist it, and even more so to fight against it. But those are high level challenges, not expected of everyone.

A PERSPECTIVE SHIFT

As a young person learning about twentieth century history, I struggled to make sense of it, I wondered what I was doing living on such a planet. It struck me as so barbaric, pointless and inhumane. These sentiments were summarised in the famous line of Theodor Adorno, *"After Auschwitz it is impossible to write poetry"*. The physical world is real when we are in it, but we are also not in it, in the sense we are all spirit and this is not our natural domain. It is an artificial construct, just as the "dreamworld" was portrayed in the film *"The Matrix"* as not being the real world. What I failed to appreciate as a young man, is that we are all spirit here temporarily having an expression as a human and all here to learn through experience, about unconditional love in its positive and negative aspects. Most of the participants in Auschwitz and the other atrocities will have pre-planned the experiences they had, while in the spirit state. They will have had their individual reasons, but collectively many will have advanced their knowledge and so be able to progress along the spiritual journey.

The hope for the planet's future is having reached a nadir of spirituality, the start of the planet's ascendance has now been made and there will shortly be a leaving behind of such negative experiences as the new higher cycle of evolution is due to begin in 2012. Many who took part in Auschwitz and similar genocide events will, I suspect, be reincarnating sometime after 2012 when they will be able to obtain their growth through spiritual and harmonious experiences, and so complete their frame of reference.

Having taken on the difficult challenge of explaining Auschwitz in spiritual terms, in the next chapter I take on the perhaps more controversial challenge of showing how spirituality and religion are not to be confused with each other.

CHAPTER EIGHT

THE DIFFERENCE BETWEEN SPIRITUALITY AND RELIGION

I would like to address the confusion between spirituality and religion. They are thought of by many as being synonymous, but sometimes in fact they are poles apart. One can be spiritual without any religious practices but conversely, having religious faith and worship does not mean one has great spirituality. A necessary corollary is to consider the nature of God, since worship of some concept of God is a feature of Christianity, Judaism, Islam, and Hinduism. A second corollary is to consider ourselves in relation to what is understood by "God." We all have a good idea of what religion is, so is a definition of spirituality without religion possible? I give a channelled description of a spiritual person, a definition of the Source (or God) and briefly describe the spiritual journey, religion being only one aspect of it.

Many recognise the emptiness and the lack of purpose of secularism, but do not know what to put in its place. Channel 4 television had a programme (June 2005) for instance entitled "Spirituality Shopper." It documented a lady sampling yoga, gospel singing, Christian meditation, and helping in a Hindu temple kitchen. After a month's trial of all four, she and her live-in partner concluded she was much calmer and less stressed, and more mindful of the needs of others. One difficulty in drawing any real conclusion must be the "camera factor", that doing something knowing you are being filmed can influence results by heightening self-awareness. Another viewer imponderable is what material was edited out before being broadcast, as any extremely favourable or unfavourable viewpoint may have been in order to avoid the accusation of bias or the giving of offence.

OUR SPIRITUAL AGES

Spirituality does not have to be sought. We are all a spiritual being first and foremost, a human person is our temporary expression, a human body the container for the spirit or soul. There are degrees of spirituality exhibited by people, which is primarily a reflection of their spiritual age and nothing immediately to do with following any religion. To recap, there are five ages or levels to the spiritual journey. Beginner or young spirit are level one. Old or experienced spirit are level fives. Planet Earth is mostly occupied by level one spirit. This makes it by definition the "nursery world" of the universe. It is the planet spirit uses for experiences appropriate for young spirit. Part of those experiences are those of having religious beliefs and devotion, part of the much bigger syllabus to learn what love is.

Our time spent as homo sapiens is only a part of our total experiences. On more advanced worlds than Earth, there is no religion as we understand it here. They have worked through those experiences and left them behind. They have knowledge of the true nature of spirit and its workings. They have their religious experience in their memories as the contrast or the comparison to what are the spiritual truths. Religious experiences are valid and necessary, but they are more commonly experienced by young spirit, and a feature of the lives of such spirit.

That is not to say old spirit cannot return to the nursery world and have religious experiences. They do, partly to complete their experiences if there is a gap in that aspect of them, and secondly to use religion as a means to achieve some other missing experience. This is not for religion's own sake but possibly as guide, tutor, and leader for others. Pope John Paul II for example was an old spirit. His was a life of sincerely held beliefs, but his life's purpose was not to advance Catholicism, but to help others through his role as religious leader, and to have the experience of that. As we recall, Catholicism was instrumental in Poland in bringing about an end to Communist rule. That was John Paul's life purpose, or rather a part of it, to use Christian ideology as a means to overthrow another ideology, that of Communism.

In the incarnated state, spirituality can be likened to the transformation from a demanding needful, totally dependent human baby to that of a mature adult one who hopefully will be

127

thoughtful, loving, humane, unselfish and so on (not all are). A newly separated spirit is a little like a human baby. It has not yet learned about life. A baby is only capable of thinking of and expressing its own needs. A mature adult may also be capable of considering the needs of others, may be creative, and may work for the greater good and so on. It is really miraculous that these changes should occur. If a piece of computer software were subjected to human life experiences, it would still be the same before and afterwards. A soul is capable of refinement; indeed it is constructed in such a way that higher versions of itself can be activated.

This transformation from no spirituality to fully so is by small increments and requires many lifetimes to be complete. Our evidence for this is to observe the differences in people of similar biological age in their attitude and behaviour. If this transformation were merely a result of the passage of time in a single lifetime, we would all arrive at having an equal amount of humanity or compassion. Clearly we do not. The explanation is not one of different birth circumstances and nurturing, since there are plenty of examples of people rising above humble origins or trying times as a youngster to become outstanding as an adult in their compassion, morality, virtue and so on. Indeed, it is amazing when one considers how children from the same family and upbringing sometimes turn out so completely different. The answer is primarily the result of different life-plans and spiritual-age variation.

The overarching explanation for differences in responses and attitude between people is their spiritual age. We vary greatly in our spiritual ages, which in turn is the product of the number of lives we have already lived in the body. There are thus degrees of spirituality. A beginner has little. A spiritual master has a full quota, being a spirit that has incarnated many times and has learned through practical experience all the many and varied aspects of "unconditional love". (To give an illustration of differences, George Bush is a level one spirit; Nelson Mandela is a level five.) At the end of the chapter I use the 9/11 tragedy to further illustrate differences in attitudes.

A NEW WORD FOR GOD

To understand spirituality in its true sense, not the one distorted
by religious connotations, it helps to understand what God is, and
his purpose. The reason for the popularity of the *"Conversations
with God"* and subsequent books by Neale Donald Walsch is to
redefine God for those in the West whose mindset is fixed by
Christian notions of what God is. The popularity of Dan Brown's
"The Da Vinci Code", is to help unseat the centuries of Christian
ideology, aimed at control of the people by censorship and
manipulation of spiritual truths.

A more descriptive term for God, one used by higher life-forms
elsewhere in the universe, is "the Collective." This also more easily
allows us to embrace the notion that, each and everyone of us, and
all other living things as well, are part of the Collective. All come
from the Source or One, and all return at some point to it. The
religious teachings of the hurdles to leap, behaviour to adopt,
rituals to perform, and so on, are irrelevant to the certainty all
will return to the Source, irrespective of their thoughts or
behaviour patterns. That is not to say there is no purpose or
benefit to ritual, as there can be inner peace from some practices.
It is just to say it is a human misconception, and often a human
means of control, to believe a return to Source cannot be achieved
without certain beliefs and practices.

The ultimate conspiracy theory is that biological life is the only
form of life. This is not the real world. To arrive at that realisation
is not easy. We are largely limited to knowledge of the territory by
the map our five body senses create. As many have pointed out the
map is not the territory. If we lack mediumship skill or psychic
awareness, we lack the vital sensor that tells us the physical world
is not the whole story, that there are other dimensions, and indeed
the existence of the physical world originates in those dimensions.
We are the *"Matrix"* paradigm in reverse: the dream world creates
the physical one but instead of machines of artificial intelligence
doing so, it is spirit that does. To be in the spirit state is normal; to
be incarnated is the exception.

THE SYLLABUS

Before any human life exists it is planned in the spirit state. As spirit, or consciousness as some call the soul, we inhabit the spirit realms prior to finding ourselves in the biological container we call the human body. When that expires we return to the spirit dimensions. Why then do we take the trouble to be here? To rediscover in the physical form the spirituality we have in the spirit state. This is the game of life. It is based around a syllabus to fully explore "unconditional love".

It was set up by the Collective so that it would know itself through experiences. Religions are one small aspect of the total syllabus of experiences established by the Collective. They form the contrast to what the spiritual truths are in some cases. Religions contain various degrees of distortion concerning spiritual concepts. They share a common element in being originated by one person's philosophy, that then adopted by others, then variations applied through the generations. One might say they contain human error, but intentionally so, since spiritually speaking, nothing happens by accident. Religions are "introduced" on a nursery world to provide the backdrop or stage prop for certain dramas to occur. In turn these allow various subplots to be written.

An important stage prop use for religion concerns a particular aspect of "unconditional love", that of "acceptance of difference, faith and belief". To experience this aspect one needs clearly a faith or belief system, and then to take a contrary opinion, or no opinion. In another scenario, a belief system can be used to violently oppose non-acceptance; hence the religious wars through history. This continues today in Muslim fundamentalism. One can use both sides of this non-acceptance as experience opportunities; the zealot and the sufferer of others religious zeal. Both learn about this aspect of love. As with all lives, most of the learning will probably take place in the life-review back in spirit rather than during the life itself.

Any ideology can be the circumstance or stage prop to experience this aspect, not just religion. It abounds in civil wars, when family members may take opposing viewpoints. It need not always be associated with violence – ethnic tension and racial minority intolerance are opportunities for verbal non-acceptance of differences, the more common situation in recent times.

I fully describe the syllabus in chapter nine. I give here a list of the main headings so it can be seen how wide the concept of love is: Parental love as parent and as child; sibling love; family love; friendship; environmental love; humanitarianism; tutoring; romantic love; life partnership; love of identity; self-love; love of home; love of pets; grief; religious fervour and worship. These are the main aspects. Each one has many subheadings and those may be experienced in their positive aspects and their negative.

SPIRITUAL AWARENESS

There are a number of basic premises to spiritual awareness. These include: we reincarnate, we have a life-plan and we have a spirit guide. Are these not the foundation for another belief system like religion? They are supported by evidence, albeit indirect or circumstantial at times. (I discuss each in detail in other writings.) Awareness has to be arrived at by the individual for himself. The difference between spiritual truths and religion is that spiritual truths need to be found. They are not taught or inculcated by a culture, as is religion. If they are, then acceptance of something by rote or through peer pressure, or childhood conditioning is not achievement or discovery, and therefore spiritual progression. This has form but not substance; it is speaking words without knowing their meaning.

We have lives on a planet such as Earth currently is, precisely because of the absence of knowledge here, and what little knowledge there is has become distorted. It thus constitutes a challenge to become spiritually aware. We handicap ourselves to increase the difficulty. One of the ways older spirit will sometimes do this is to allow themselves to be educated in religious beliefs and practices and then see if their rational mind will reject those beliefs, and if their true spirituality will replace a manmade world view.

Let us examine my basic premise, the fact that we reincarnate. In a Western Culture there is as yet little acceptance, but knowledge of it makes a huge difference to our view of life and massively informs our view of others. It diminishes fear of death, fear of other people; it makes a nonsense of violence and enmity because when we reincarnate it is into many and varied cultures. There can be no enemies since we are all one. How spiritual is that, and how unlike those current Americans who are militaristic but at the same time "put their trust in God"? It is no coincidence, the religion with most acceptance of reincarnation (not the same as personal discovery of it) is also the one that preaches non-violence, Buddhism. In contrast, for some of their followers religions without acceptance of reincarnation, Christianity and Islam, have historically and today found no contradiction between violence and devotion to their beliefs.

LIFE-PLANS

Let us consider my second basic premise, that we each have a life-plan. In that knowledge, spirituality is the potential for growth in following our life-plan, whatever that may be. A life-plan is composed in spirit before our arrival. At its core is experiences chosen appropriate for the spiritual age concerning furthering knowledge of some aspect of "unconditional love", both in its positive version and its negative. Therefore, whilst on the face of it, a circumstance or experience can seem far removed from what is commonly thought of as "spiritual", such an experience will be intended for the lessons it can teach, and by helping to build a much bigger picture, therefore be in fact, spiritual.

That can at times be hard to see from the human angle and needs the higher perspective to do so. Often we need to turn a situation around and ask what does this person require spiritually? Let us take the case of conspicuous consumption – The example of the English footballer and his wife, affectionately known as Posh and Becks, come to mind, but it applies to many whose destiny is to acquire and display wealth. There is no point spiritually in being a millionaire, except the one to experience that very point! The riches we may acquire on Earth are not riches of the spirit or soul, although our culture might suggest they are. Once returned to spirit, all will realise that wealth on Earth, is just that, wealth on

Earth. The riches of spirit, for example, are the inner battles that have been fought and knowledge gained, the achievements made in the face of opposition and the unselfish help given to others.

Recognising that money is a false God is a huge challenge in a culture that revolves principally around it. For an older spirit, the challenge might be to have it in one's life-plan to become wealthy and then experience the test of philanthropy. Depak Chopra has a dictum, "You only get to keep what you give away". I conclude what he means is that we accrue spiritual growth through using our wealth for the benefit of others. The Christian teaching about a rich man having great difficulty entering the Kingdom of Heaven (camel and eye of a needle) is not true. The correct basis to it is that being rich can be a barrier to spiritual growth since discomfort is often required to seek wisdom. In addition, there is no emotion usually (except fear of losing wealth) associated with having riches. It is through emotional experiences, both painful and joyful, that we grow spiritually. What the teaching ought to say is that dying with riches gains one little in spiritual terms. That is not to say poverty of itself is spiritual, since either extreme is a barrier to spiritual awareness.

Nearly everything in life takes place as the result of a pre-planned intention. There are two lines of script in the film *"Matrix Reloaded"* that ought to be put on all hymn books, prayer books and religious and philosophical reference books. These are the words spoken to the character Neo by the Oracle, "You didn't come here to make the choice... You've already made it. You are here to understand why you have made it". This is a reference to the life-plan made before incarnation.

Just as no actor or actress will walk on a stage without having memorised a script, no spirit incarnates as a human without a life-plan except we forget the life-plan on arrival. The role of the spirit guide is to help us find our destiny, to fulfil the life-plan. The guide will not make decisions for us because we have a measure of free-will. Indeed recognising on some level what is the better decision spiritually (not on a human level) is one further test we build into the plan. Sometimes a decision can lead to hardships and suffering, or lead us to commit an act and feel guilt, or not as the case may be.

Crossroads or major decision points are a feature of life-plans. They were neatly epitomised in the blue pill/red pill situation in the film *"The Matrix"*. Had Neo taken the blue pill, he would not have achieved his destiny (or more correctly, if every time he was offered a pill, he took the blue one as key decisions will have repeat opportunities in the plan). The consequence would be a repeat life, since all must experience everything at some point on the spiritual journey. Taking the red pill led him to much suffering and agonising, but huge spiritual growth. His destiny was exceptional because he was an old spirit. The tasks and challenges we face in incarnation are graded according to our spiritual age.

Where is the spiritual purpose, one might ask, in say being diagnosed with a serious or terminal illness? The two overt connections between such illness and religion that come to mind are, firstly to prompt a person to contemplate their mortality and seek religious beliefs, and secondly the Buddhist concept of Karma, that somehow we brought about the illness through past actions. Spiritually there is a myriad of reasons why one might choose illness as part of a life-plan. It is not possible to generalise except to say the emotions experienced by the sufferer or those close, or both, will be the spiritual reasoning. Illness is an intended event in the vast majority of cases. It is predetermined as part of a life-plan. It is a "popular" choice because so much growth can be obtained using it as a tool or prop in life's play. Have you noticed the changes in a person who has suffered serious illness (or indeed other trauma)? Sometimes their outlook on life changes radically, and from that, their behaviour towards others.

We are familiar with the notion of "death bed conversions" to a faith. One scenario involving illness might be a death bed realisation of spiritual concepts, a little late in life but nevertheless arriving at them whilst in the body, which all will do at some point. This is a challenge that will feature not once, but several times on the spiritual journey of many lives, with increasing depths of understanding each time the goal or intended outcome, and not necessarily on a death bed, but at earlier times in the life.

Another example of a situation that may appear far removed from spirituality is serious drug addiction. Such a condition or experience will again be a tool to learn about some aspect of unconditional love. For example, about self love. One may intentionally have a lack of self-esteem and as a consequence turn to hard drugs. That may be for the experience itself, for the challenge of rescuing oneself from it, or for the opportunity of ones close to still love without condition. Another use of the same tool is to learn respect for and care of one's body. To allow drugs to abuse one's health can either be for that experience or again, for the challenge of recovering oneself from it. The same prop can have many different purposes depending where one is on the spiritual journey.

One could generalise and say there is spiritual purpose in all life experiences, no matter what they are. Sometimes the purpose will seem obscure but will be known in spirit. It will be made clear on return to spirit as all of us review our lives once we are back there. For young spirit, in particular, that is where most learning takes place. Unlike Neo, they are not expected to understand the choices during the life. The spiritual lessons learned and growth achieved are easier to understand in the spirit state than when in physical incarnation. What may seem a failure in human terms, can be a success spiritually because of what has been learnt. We should not judge or jump to conclusions. Life-plans are a vast topic, which I have only touched upon here, in order to define spirituality as knowledge gained through chosen experiences.

SPIRITUALITY IS A WAY OF LIFE

A small but revealing everyday indicator of spirituality and the different degrees of it exhibited by humans is this. When driving on a motorway or dual carriageway, I travel often at the permitted legal speed limit. On numerous occasions a vehicle will pull out in front of me to overtake, ignoring my fast approach from behind. Sometimes I am obliged to brake sharply. This lack of consideration is a low level spirit behaviour. Sometimes, but less frequently, I notice a vehicle will wait until the rear is clear before over-taking. A more evolved spirit. Spirituality has been described as "a way of life". Certainly consideration for others is not something all people are equally capable of exhibiting. The degree of it is an indicator of spiritual age. Another small illustration of lack of spirituality is those who throw litter from their cars or drop litter. Care of the environment is an aspect of love. Disrespect for it is an equally valid experience but not one we hopefully learn to prefer.

A less trivial illustration of variation in incarnated spirituality is the different attitude to children shown by divorced or separated parents. One party may insist on 95% of the "contact", never facilitate the other partner seeing the children, use the child maintenance as their own meal ticket, never remind the children to telephone or email the absent parent and so on. Just a one-sided declaration of needs and an inability to put oneself in the shoes of another and think, "how would I like it if the situation were reversed?" A low level spirit is not capable of moving as far beyond the human baby's self-centredness, as is an older spirit. (There is no ethical or moral judgement in this example. It may or may not be in the life-plan of the deprived parent to experience separation from ones children – an equally valid spiritual experience as is a close bond. Duality or contrast is a fundamental of acquiring knowledge. The self-centred parent will hopefully see the error in their behaviour in their life review, the deprived parent will better understand parental love through being denied its expression.)

The purpose of all experiences throughout progression is to illustrate the concept of love and to further our understanding of it. In order to know what "love" is there are many aspects to explore, consideration for others being only one of them. They include: compassion, sympathy, empathy and kindness; respect, admiration, esteem, support and approval; understanding, perception, encouragement, trust; encouragement of growth and self-respect; care, concern and education; tolerance, forbearance and patience; charity and reason; acceptance of difference, faith and belief; conviction, approbation and appreciation; peace, harmony, amity and freedom from strife; delight in prosperity and success. These aspects to be fully understood may need to be experienced in both a positive way and a negative one. So, for example, compassion may be experienced as given, as received, as absent when it ought to be given or received, and in its opposite as anger, hostility and so on.

THE ALL THAT IS

I would now like to consider the crux question: what is God? Different religions have their unique interpretations. Some, such as Buddhism, do not really embrace the notion as central to their teaching. At the risk of a "fatwa", I put forward this understanding: everything that exists is energy in one form or another. The Creator, God, Universal Architect, or my preferred term, the Collective, is an intense concentration of communication energy. Communication energy is one of the seven components of universal energy, which is found everywhere in the universe. In the stars, the planets, the moons. All living things, to be alive must receive universal energy. In one sense therefore, God is all that there is.

The Collective is all knowledge, all life, all planning, all education, all love, all everything. Everything that exists in incarnation, even life itself, is by grace of the Collective. It provides every element of universal energy; it provides the platform for every piece of universal knowledge that spirit has; it provides the means of incarnation; it lays the framework and provides the network of energy necessary for all life wherever it occurs. It knows all and is all; it is the source; the beginning and end for each on the spiritual journey.

THE JOURNEY

What then is the spiritual journey? A graduate after three or more years of study and mental effort has thirty seconds of recognition and fame in the degree award ceremony. I regret to say, the spiritual journey is somewhat akin to that. The syllabus of study is already established and laid out. It was compiled by the Collective. The student has to be willing to undertake the study, to want to further individual knowledge and understanding. In spirit all students, or souls, know what "unconditional love" is. When they experience communication from the Collective, the vibration felt is that of unconditional love. That is the feeling of being in the spirit state. Their task is to know what that is by direct experiences. Each student collects experiences and like a bee depositing nectar on return to the hive after visiting many flowers, so each spirit offers its experiences of many different and varied lifetimes on many planets. Those experiences are given to the Collective so it may know itself better. The student receives the equivalent of thirty seconds of fame. After completing the journey, the disc is wiped clean, as it were, and a new journey begins after spending a period of time within the Collective. This is a never-ending cycle.

Each one of us on planet Earth, and those on the seventy-four other planets used by spirit in this universe, is at a particular point on this journey, which has thirty-five stages to it (thirty-six if one includes that of "spiritual master". This is a spirit that has completed the journey but has two further incarnations of choice). I have known some people when being told of their stage, have feelings of inferiority that they are not the oldest of spirit. This is a human problem as we can be obsessed by rank and status. Spiritually all are equal. Just because one may be a young spirit now, and another an old one, is not to deny the young spirit may have "been around the block" more often, so how does one define young and old? Time is not an issue in spirit, so one cannot claim any superiority in speed of completion. If anything, the least number of repeat lives necessary might be a measure of spiritual success. There is no honours degree or grading of results. All spirit graduate in due course, with equal status.

As others have said also, there is no judgement back in the spirit state. We judge ourselves, and arrive at our own conclusions. Young spirit do receive help and guidance from older spirit, but it is still true to say, each must arrive at their own opinion of what is preferred and what is not, of what is good and what is evil. That is an earthly term. Evil cannot exist in the spirit state, but can be observed and experienced in the incarnated form. This is for the purpose of forming a frame of reference, to know love in both its positive and negative versions. In order to create a drama, to provide challenge, there is intentionally opposition in life, which we might sometimes refer to as "evil". In the *"Matrix"* trilogy, agent Smith and Neo are opposites. They are expressions of the same energy, which is why one cannot destroy the other. They are different polarities of that energy. Through a tension of opposites, we create a tragedy drama.

Spirituality can be measured if we must, by how much of the syllabus has been completed so far. It has as its reward or compensation, progression through the planes or dimensions we can occupy in the natural spirit state. One cannot progress in the spirit realms without incarnating and having experiences. No pain, no gain is true spirituality as well as bodily in certain human situations, as pain acts a tutor in our learning and growth. All spirit, I am told, have an innate wish to return to Source, which motivates them.

THE RELIGION DIMENSION TO LOVE

The purpose of this chapter is to address the confusion between spirituality and religion. Realising that the two are quite different is one of the items under the heading "religion", which in turn is one aspect only of experiencing unconditional love. I would like to quote in detail that aspect of the syllabus. It has the following headings, each of which can be experienced from different perspectives:

a) The foremost aspect of love from this heading is faith and belief, both of which are given blindly by religious followers in the main.
b) Trust in religious leaders.
c) Betrayal of trust by religious leaders.
d) Reliance on religion to provide a framework for one's life rather than following inner knowledge.
e) Blindly following someone else's vision rather than your own.
f) Reliance on the policy of others without understanding the question.

g) Disempowering oneself by giving power to religious representatives.

h) Control! Control! Control!

i) Dogma and doctrine more important in religion than spirituality.

j) Used as a vehicle for self-advancement of the few.

k) Used by many to obtain feelings of superiority over one's fellow man.

l) Lacking in true love and spirituality.

m) Obsession with the material – churches, trappings etc.

n) Church uses wealth for self, not for populace.

o) True spirituality has no relationship to religion.

p) Recognition of spiritual truths and that religions are man made.

q) Recognition that choice of creed is not worth killing each other for as we are all spirit beings and may reincarnate as a member of the despised religion in our future lives.

r) Superiority practised by priests over the people.

"Control" is the major characteristic of religion. When the Romans removed references to reincarnation from the early Christian bible when they adopted it in around AD350, it was an early example of the church and state making common cause for mutual benefit. A belief in reincarnation would lessen deference towards the hierarchy. Was it a mere coincidence that the Normans in Britain often built a castle in close proximity to their cathedrals? If thought control of the people failed, the backup of the threat or use of force was the alternative. In the Middle Ages, the papal army was not an oxymoron, but an actual fighting force. How does one remotely begin to explain the Spanish Inquisition or the Reign of Terror, except in the negative, to teach us what are not the spiritual truths? As such these were intended events in the world plan.

The reader will be able no doubt to relate their personal experiences to some of the above headings, or relate their knowledge of history and world events to them. There are two items in the newspapers recently. The Residential Institutions Redress Board in Ireland was set up in 2002 and to date has received 7,046 applications for financial compensation. The average award is £52,300. In total nine thousand people are expected to apply and payment could cost £680 million. The cases include physical cruelty and emotional abuse by nuns and sisters of the Catholic Church in the 1940s and 1950s in residential schools. (An example of betrayal of trust.) Many observers in their obituaries of him noted the major disappointment of Pope John Paul II was his failure to overcome the conservative forces in the Church to overturn the ruling on contraception. Many thousands need not have suffered the Aids virus, a momentous example of both religion's control and the giving away of personal freedom by adherents.

The antonym of control is "empowerment". That is a useful test between what is spirituality and what is religion. If someone empowers you, they are behaving spiritually. If someone disempowers you in the context of faith and belief, they have another agenda, possibly financial or possibly egotistical, by creating a following or subservience. As yet another challenge to finding the spiritual truths, there can be red herrings or false trails on the route. This may include encountering people or organisations that on the surface appear to offer the longed-for answers and means to inner peace, but create a dependency. Those that get caught up in them, will have done so for the lessons it will teach, as with orthodox religion.

A SPIRITUAL PERSON

I would like to give this channelled description of what is a spiritual person. It is reached after many lifetimes of learning about love in all its aspects, the spiritual baby having become the spiritual senior citizen:

- fine, noble and high-minded
- kind, generous, giving, charitable, munificent and bountiful
- dignified, honourable and gracious
- decent, righteous, virtuous, pure, moral and upright
- worthy, ethical, just and principled
- wholesome, civilised and courteous
- enlightened, loving and devout

- open, benevolent, thoughtful and humane.

Clearly, this has little connection at all with the special clothing and ornate buildings, a hierarchy of devotees, instructions handed from the few to the many, adherence to ancient writings, and the other attributes of what is commonly thought of as "religion". Nor is it something that can be obtained through a month's trial purchase that the lady "Spirituality Shopper" in the TV documentary seemed to suggest.

THE FUTURE

I would like to refer to Hannah Beaconsfield's channelled vision of the future of religion, "The metamorphosis of religion in the new millennium" chapter of her book *"Riding the Phoenix"*. This is the prediction that organised religion will change to an internalised personal religious experience. This will be in loose groupings of similar minded people. When people realise we are each a tiny part of the Creator, and we are connected not separated with the Source, then many of the existing illusions about ourselves and life on Earth will disappear. We disempower ourselves by allowing others to claim superiority. "The only authority of the future will be the inner voice of the God-self. All personal experience will be filtered through this lens before it is accepted by the individual," she writes. Recognising that we are all equal spirits is fundamental to the new world. Each human being is a Temple of God. Everyone will be seen as a House of God, in which each individual is free to blossom and to experience whatever it is they have chosen. The inner wisdom and progression so far attained will make those choices the higher ones for most spirits. Nursery world experiences can then be confined to the next nursery world, allowing this one to be a more highly evolved planet.

These new practices will be different for each person according to their spiritual age. The future scenarios I have just described are more likely those of middle-aged spirits. Old spirit would more likely be in regular and intense contact with the spirit realms, individually or perhaps in pairs, with their soul twin. There will be a return to the recognition of the special places where there is a concentration of universal energies, and these will be used more as meeting points, where the energies allow easier spirit communication and facilitate a feeling of connectedness. There will be a return to celebration of cosmic and planetary cycles.

The ultimate spiritual experience, the one we lose memory of in incarnation, but have memory of in the spirit state, is that of the feeling of being part of the Collective, and feeling what the Collective feels. It is the consciousness of being the universe, being all things, the stars, the galaxies, and of oneness. It is the memory of this feeling that "drives" spirit to wish to return back to the womb, that motivates spirit to make the considerable efforts required to undertake the spiritual journey of experiences back to the Source. That is the purpose of our existence here and elsewhere. It is given to few individuals to have in the body recall of what it is to feel that oneness. Those that do begin to understand how all the joy, pain, sorrow, elation, guilt and happiness we feel as part of humanity have purpose. We are knowing ourselves through experiences, exposure to religions being only one category of them.

In the next chapter I document the complete syllabus of unconditional love as we can relate to it on Earth. Before that I would like to tabulate the differing attitudes in relation to one event with possible spiritual age against each. Wisdom comes with spiritual age, not biological age. An explanation for being misunderstood is spiritual age variation with those in our immediate circle. In the extreme, this can be a feeling of just not belonging on this planet at all.

THE DIFFERENCE BETWEEN SPIRITUALITY AND RELIGION

THE EXAMPLE OF THE 9/11 TRAGEDY AND DIFFERENT ATTITUDES TOWARDS IT

Attitude	Possible Spiritual Age
1. A terrorist outrage of the most vile kind.	LEVEL ONE – surface conclusion quickly drawn.
2. An act of war that demands vengeance and bringing the culprits "to justice." (i.e. death)	LEVEL ONE – an eye for an eye response.
3. The Muslim God is stronger than the capitalist Christian God. The highjackers are in heaven now.	LEVEL TWO – religious extremist attitude of violence being justifiable.
4. The USA is greedy and exploits the world's resources and so brought this attack on itself.	LEVEL TWO – ideological view, immorality justifying violence.
5. The poor passengers, office workers and firemen who died innocently through no fault of their own.	LEVEL THREE – compassionate, seeing people not causes, individuals not cultures.

6. This is an act without proper cause but why do some people hate the USA so much? The highjackers are misguided and must have been brainwashed.

LEVEL THREE – attempting to rationalise the event, but seeing fault on one side only.

7. Why did the vast and costly intelligence services not warn us? Why did our highly technological armed forces not stop this?

LEVEL THREE – the search for rational – scientific answers in an industrial military culture.

8. There is a conspiracy to deceive the public about exactly what was known in advance, and there was a hidden agenda ("The New Pearl Harbour")

LEVEL FOUR – morally probing. Unaccepting of the analysis and statements by politicians.

9. Did we bring this on ourselves? We should not rush to judge the perpetrators and seek to better understand their motives.

LEVEL FOUR – ethical, not seeking revenge but understanding. Looking at the others viewpoint.

10. The USA has a disproportionate share of the world's wealth which it does little to share. It consumes energy and other resources based on economic power not on any moral principles of equality in entitlement to share in resources.

LEVEL FIVE – seeing a message in the event, the imbalance in consumption and the lack of spirituality in the West.

11. The knee-jerk response of war against Afghanistan will only cause further problems. It will not end terrorism, merely enflame it. The way to deal with terrorism is to change beliefs by teaching mankind is all one, we are all spirit first and foremost.

LEVEL FIVE – spiritual philosophy.

12. That one man, a President, or a very small group, a cabinet, can take decisions affecting the many, of going to war against Iraq with no proven link, is not democracy but disempowerment of the people and the giving away of individual responsibility.

HIGH LEVEL FIVE – spiritual philosophy.

This is a somewhat speculative table, and is not a conclusive indicator of spiritual age for each view. It is a suggestion of what attitude is likely for a certain age. There is a spectrum of possible responses to 9/11 and some of these I hope to have sequenced in terms of their spirituality for the purpose of showing how spiritual age affects opinion.

Level one spirit are unlikely to spend energy on seeking deeper meaning, would be quick to apportion blame, and see no contradiction in responding to violence with violence. Level two spirit would see events in terms of their preconceived world-views, which may include those based on dogma. Level three spirit would possibly see complexity where others see simplicity, would seek a rational rather than an emotional analysis. Level four spirit would include the contrarians, those not always following orthodoxy and the popular view. Level five spirit might look beyond surface appearances and would be the philosophers.

Level one spirit are the majority in number on Earth, hence George Bush was re-elected on a pro-war stance. It is interesting that the two British politicians who resigned over the Iraq war, the late Robin Cook and Claire Short, were the oldest spirits in the British cabinet, both level four.

CHAPTER NINE

THE SYLLABUS OF UNCONDITIONAL LOVE

"We are not sent into this world for nothing, we are not born at random: we are not here that we may go to bed at night and get up in the morning, toil for our bread, eat and drink, laugh and joke, rear a family and die. God sees every one of us, He creates every soul for a purpose."

So spoke Cardinal Newman in a sermon of 1849. His statement is empowering and spiritual, not controlling and threatening consequences for wrong behaviour. He was, I imagine, an old spirit, having chosen religion as the stage prop for his life experiences. His thoughts were on the way to understanding why we are here, but apart from that first and most critical step, that of purpose, he could perhaps elaborate no further. I was in that same position after five years on a spiritual quest. Now after a further five years, ones of spirit communication, either directly or by proxy, I am able to take a second step and say in detail what is the mission we are engaged upon.

One greatly limiting influence on Cardinal Newman's philosophy was the church dogma that we have only one lifetime. When we look in the mirror we see this lifetime's looks only. We do not see all the other versions of ourselves that have existed and are stored in our spirit memories. We can see them if we wish in our natural spirit state. For now we can only rely on the skills of the talented past life portrait artists to show us. Alternatively, we may see ourselves in a past life regression experience, the nearest thing to proof we can have of the spiritual journey.

Until recent times, children born in "civilised" societies with past life memory, had it suppressed because it was not considered acceptable. Today, there is an increasing number of children with knowledge of both past lives and life elsewhere. These children have the inner wisdom that there is continuity of life, that there is not death of the soul or spirit, that each one of us contains an element of the divine. Reaching acceptance of reincarnation is the gateway to the garden of understanding life's meaning. One then needs to be aware of life-plans, of the spiritual journey that consists of stages and levels, and finally the syllabus of experiences that make up "unconditional love".

Our culture inculcates an attitude of scepticism that keeps many people trapped in a particular mind-set and world-view. Science has, to a large extent, replaced religion as the major influence on thought and "truth". Science can be shown to have its limits. For example, healing brought about by alternative and complementary therapies defies orthodox explanation. Many more people are becoming open to healing, and are benefiting from it. This can be a major avenue to lead to a reversal of the denial of our true spiritual nature and the continuity of life for those that go on afterwards, to find out more about the workings of spirit.

Whether someone finds his or her own spiritual truth at this time depends on it being in their life-plan to do so. For the majority on Earth, that will not be the case including frustratingly sometimes, one's partner. What we frequently encounter in personal readings and in our workshops, is a marriage where one partner (usually, but not exclusively the wife) is hungry to develop his or her spirituality and the other has no interest or even puts up objection and opposition.

We have been told that spiritual beliefs only have relevance if they are arrived at by the individual for his or herself. This is why the sceptic who seeks evidence as a means of persuasion does not usually receive it. Likewise, there is no merit in one partner adopting them to satisfy the other, because they will not really believe but just be paying lip service to the ideas. One has to arrive at one's own perception of spiritual truth and not adopt someone else's without analysis or question. For those in a relationship with a mismatch of acceptance and understanding, the best that can be striven for is for one partner to be allowed to pursue his or her own beliefs without interference. The one should not try to convince the other or this may result in frustration for both. If one party is able to show tolerance for the belief of another, that is a first spiritual step in progression itself.

LIFE-PLANS

Today, more and more people are coming to realise that they and the universe are not here by chance, that there is a design to all life and certain things happen for a reason, difficult as that can sometimes be to spot. Those inner feelings about a design or inner purpose to life are a vital clue.

The cornerstone to understanding the meaning of life is life-plan. Nobody is born without a life-plan being in place beforehand. No life-plan, no life! That seems a bold statement and controversial to those who believe man makes his own history and has freewill choice. So, where is my evidence? I usually answer with another unproven statement, that we suffer temporary amnesia on incarnation, so are not consciously aware of the plan we composed for ourselves. This is a little like starting to play a game having just thrown away the rulebook! There are clues to the existence of a life-plan if one is able to spot them. I have set out fourteen possible ways to see the plan in my "Life Plan Identikit" in my book, "*Nothing Happens by Accident*".

One of these clues is an inner knowledge. This reveals itself sometimes in childhood as an early choice of career. A young person who cannot, one might think, have much knowledge of the ways of the adult world, can have a certainty of where their future lies. I was struck by the story, for example, of the butler to the late Princess Diana, Paul Burrell, being taken to Buckingham Palace by is parents when aged eight. Standing outside the gates he said, "*I am going to work there one day*". His inner knowledge was triggered by the location.

Similarly, one of the ladies at a recent workshop we hosted told me this about herself. At age six, she told her mother she wanted to be a nurse. Her parents did not take her seriously. When aged nine and at home because of illness, instead of attending school, she watched a TV programme concerning childbirth. She told her mother afterwards that she wanted to be a midwife. Her mother had been alarmed to discover she had watched what she thought was an unsuitable programme and discouraged her thoughts of such a career. When I met her she was a housewife, but told me she had previously trained as a midwife. She was now on a spiritual path and fully accepted her life was planned out before she came here. She was conscious now of receiving communication from her guide. She had, for example, designed a web site for a healing centre knowing it had a future purpose but not sure exactly in what way. We confirmed by mediumship that she had a destiny to establish a full-time healing practice.

A life-plan is a little like a stage play. There will be a main plot and various subplots. Actors and actresses will have their times for entry and departure. The chances are quite likely that some of the key or most important people in one's life will have been encountered before in previous lives. This is because in choosing supporting cast for our "play", we have a tendency to choose those we have "worked with" previously. Some will bring pain to us and others will bring joy; there will be the "evil villains" and the "fairy godmothers".

Shakespeare was a spiritual master whose life purpose was to give us subliminal spiritual truths in his plays. Many will be familiar with perhaps his most famous lines of all:

All the world's a stage
All the men and women merely players.
They have their exits and their entrances.

(Note the great poet said "exits" before and not after "entrances", making an indirect reference to reincarnation.)

Now, what is the purpose of this play? It is the means to come to know what "unconditional love" is. The following is how this was explained to us which I repeat from my first book *"Why Come Back?"*

- ❖ Spiritual progression is the means by which spiritual knowledge is acquired;
- ❖ Spiritual knowledge consists of "love";

❖ The purpose of all the experiences throughout progression are to illustrate the concept of love and to further our understanding of it.

Remember please, love is only the word used in the absence of an Earthly word suitable to convey the concept. Spirit does not need us to experience the particular emotions and incidents, or to complete tasks, just to have them to illustrate and to bring us to an understanding of the "knowledge" which is "love".

Let us start in reverse, with the end result and work backwards. The end result, the whole reason for all of it, is the enrichment of the Collective. The Collective is all, everything and has been forever, but in order to be enriched, spirit entities leave it, form a three, commence a spiritual journey and return.

Now, one must have the nature and purpose of this spiritual journey clear in one's mind at the outset of the journey. Each three have "all spiritual knowledge" immediately upon splitting from the Collective; the aim of the journey is to experience it. It is as if they know the words, but the words have no significance, they do not understand the true meaning of them until they have completed the journey then the words will have FULL meaning. This is the reason for undertaking the journey, to experience, to put meat to the bones and so be enrichment to the Collective on return.

In order to achieve this experience certain lessons have to be learned, negative as well as positive ones, and tasks undertaken illustrating the true nature of this spiritual knowledge which we call love in our language for want of a closer description. These lessons cover a series of five levels with seven stages to each level. The higher you go the greater your capacity for grasping the spiritual concept of love, which is so much larger than our Earthly concept of romantic love. This journey may have taken thousands of our years, but in spirit there is no time measured, all is now.

The difficult task is to put "spiritual knowledge" into words in a language that has no word that describes the phenomenon. Our guide advised us at the start, to forget the concept of new romantic love, the flirting, the courtship, the emotional upheavals as two people settle down to a caring and mutually satisfying relationship. This new romantic love has no bearing on the "love" of which we speak.

The "long-term relationship" type of love does have some relevance however. A good relationship between people consists of:

- ❖ Caring and compassion
- ❖ Respect for each other
- ❖ Consideration and understanding
- ❖ Support and nurturing
- ❖ Enrichment of each others lives
- ❖ Trust and acceptance
- ❖ Encouragement and validation
- ❖ Allowing the other to grow, to be, to advance
- ❖ Encouraging their sense of worth.

In the spiritually aware, we can add the encouragement and delight in the other's spiritual progression.

Now, in adding all of this to the understanding of the word "love" when applied to mankind, the global view, some aspects repeat but are expanded while others are completely new:

- ❖ Compassion, sympathy, empathy, kindness and consideration
- ❖ Respect, admiration, esteem, support and approval
- ❖ Understanding, perception, encouragement, trust
- ❖ Encouragement of growth and self respect,
- ❖ Care, concern and education,
- ❖ Tolerance, forbearance and patience
- ❖ Charity and reason
- ❖ Acceptance of difference, faith and belief
- ❖ Conviction, approbation and appreciation
- ❖ Peace, harmony, amity and freedom from strife
- ❖ Delight in prosperity and success

In fact, many of these are, or at any rate, should be true in personal love too.

To go further, now, add to the picture your understanding of a good and loving person,

- ❖ Fine, noble and high minded
- ❖ Kind, generous, giving, charitable, munificent and bountiful,
- ❖ Dignified, honourable and gracious
- ❖ Decent, righteous, virtuous, pure, moral and upright
- ❖ Worthy, ethical, just and principled
- ❖ Wholesome, civilised and courteous
- ❖ Enlightened, spiritual, and devout
- ❖ Open, benevolent, thoughtful and humane.

Our guide advises us that this gives as full a description of spiritual love as we are likely to arrive at within the confines of our language. As you can see, far more complex than romantic hearts and flowers!

The syllabus of experiences was set out by the Creator (Higher Power, Great Spirit or other preferred term for God) in order that he could know himself through the very many parts of Himself, which we call spirits or souls, by journeying through them. I asked for a list of the different aspects of unconditional love. Our guide replied that he could not give a definitive answer as this is a very wide area, but a working list would be:

- Parental Love – Parent
- Parental Love – Child
- Sibling Love
- Family Love – (belonging, kinship)
- Friendship, Companionship and Camaraderie
- Environmental Love – (respect for nature, the planet etc)
- Humanitarianism
- Tutoring – (not in an official sense, but the giving of one's knowledge to another)
- Romantic Love
- Life Partnership
- Love of identity (national, regional, local, personal pride –

all of which needs to be learned so that it can be seen that it should be replaced with global pride)
- Self-love (self esteem, self belief, self worth, honour – so many aspects to this one)
- Love for one's home (wherever or whatever it is and for what it provides emotionally not materially!)
- Love of pets
- Respect
- Grief
- Religious fervour and worship
- Sympathy, concern and compassion
- Empathy
- Understanding, kindness and consideration
- Admiration.

Most of these can be experienced in positive and negative ways and within each is a myriad of aspects to make up the one heading. Each life-plan will have one main plot and a number of sub-plots put into a variety of settings (or stage props) revolving around an aspect of the syllabus. I believe I am most privileged to be in receipt of this information. It shows us what we all are here to experience and accomplish. A single lifetime would only allow one small aspect to be experienced, hence the spiritual journey consists of hundreds of incarnations.

The following lists are not definitive, but should form a broad outline. Of course, for most of these there are the positive and negative sides to be experienced, and then there is the lesson of "all things in balance", of not pursuing any one aspect to the detriment of others, of not letting ego take over. Every experience may be personally experienced, or via the experiences of another. The context or exact circumstances of our chosen experiences are down to our free-will choice. We may decide to use one or more world events, or we may not. We decide our nationality, gender, looks, career, hobbies, and so on.

My syllabus starts with parental love from the child's perspective. Have you ever wondered why you ended up with a particular parent, or wondered why your children turned out the way they did despite your best efforts? A spiritual explanation is that the choice of parent is made so the life-plans of both child and parent are complementary in some way. That compatibility may not be purely for joy, but also for whatever lessons one has chosen to experience. Our guide gave us an elaboration of the seemingly simple matter of parental love; first as child then as parent. He then went on to give a further list of headings to each aspect of love.

PARENTAL LOVE – CHILD

a)   Enjoying the love and support of both parents
b)   Love and support of one parent and not the other
c)   Jealousy of one parent for the love given by the other
d)   Being understood by parents
e)   Being misunderstood by parents
f)   Empathy given by parents
g)   Lack of empathy given by parents
h)   Mental connection with parent
i)   Being used as an emotional prop by a parent who should be offering support to you.
j)   Abandonment by parents, even if this is through their demise
k)   Abuse by those who should protect
l)   Neglect and indifference
m)   Sympathetic treatment by parents
n)   Consideration offered by parents
o)   Tolerance offered by parents
p)   Simple kindness from parents
q)   Deep affection for parents
r)   Devotion of parents
s)   Cruelty of parents
t)   Lack of interest of parents
u)   Feeling of responsibility for parents

PARENTAL LOVE – PARENT

a)   Love and support of one's children
b)   Indifference of one's children
c)   Estrangement from one's children

d)   An affinity with one child above others which can lead to guilt

e)   Providing enough love alone to make up for that not given by two parents, even if this is because they are absent through demise.

f)   Jealousy of the other parent for the love given to the child

g)   Using a child as a prop for one's emotions; feeling the guilt for this, or not as the case may be.

h)   Jealousy of one's children

i)   Abuse by one's children, physically or emotionally

j)   Abuse of one's children, either physically or emotionally

k)   Witnessing abuse by the other parent of one's children

l)   Neglect of, or indifference to one's children

m)   Being understood by one's children

n)   Being misunderstood by one's children

o)   Empathy given by one's children

p)   Lack of empathy given by one's children

q)   Mental connection with one's children

r)   Sympathetic treatment by one's children

s)   Consideration offered by one's children

t)   Tolerance offered by one's children

u)   Simple kindness from one's children

v)   Deep affection for one's children

w)   Devotion of one's children

x)   Cruelty of one's children

y)   Lack of interest of one's children

z)   Feeling a burden to one's children

SIBLING LOVE

a)   Natural, healthy love of a sibling

b)   Setting example to sibling

c)   Hero worship of sibling

d)   Protection of sibling against other children

e)   In adulthood, protection of sibling against other adults

f)   Feeling of responsibility for sibling

g)   Acting in loco-parentis to a sibling when parenting is lacking due to bereavement or inability of parents to offer this

h) Loss of own childhood for sibling – the need to grow up too soon so as to be able to fend for self and siblings
i) Jealousy of a sibling
j) Resentment of a sibling
k) Competition with siblings for parental love
l) Neglect of a sibling
m) Craving for love of a sibling that is withheld
n) Copying a sibling
o) Abuse of sibling – physical or emotional
p) Feeing of superiority to sibling
q) Feeling of inferiority to sibling

FAMILY LOVE

a) Pride in lineage, dynasty or ancestors
b) Bond with family members
c) Connection with family members
d) Feeling of belonging
e) Feeling of not fitting in with family
f) Rapport with family members
g) Love of family members
h) Support of family members
i) Loyalty to family members
j) Understanding and empathy for family members
k) Trust in family members
l) Steadfastness of family members
m) Disloyalty of family members
n) Constancy, dependability and reliability of family members
o) Unfaithfulness of family members
p) Losing touch with family
q) Family members in closer roles than their relationships demand – e.g. and Aunt who is more like a mother
r) Diplomacy and tact in family situations
s) Lack of diplomacy and tact in family situations
t) Speaking out for good of family even if this is against one's inclinations
u) Consideration of family members
v) Responsibility for family members

w)   Feeling of being trapped by responsibility for family members

x)   Failure to take responsibility for family members

FRIENDSHIP, COMPANIONSHIP AND CAMARADERIE

a)   Love of friend or friends
b)   Closeness to friend
c)   Identifying 'sibling-like' feelings for friend
d)   Feeling of comfort and familiarity
e)   Loyalty to friends and from friends
f)   Disloyalty of friends
g)   Comradeship and camaraderie
h)   Companionship
i)   Having someone to turn to
j)   Being someone to turn to
k)   The taking of advice from one who has your interests at heart
l)   The giving of advice to one whose interests you have at heart
m)   Like-minded, harmonious, peaceful relationships
n)   Diplomacy and tact in friendship
o)   Speaking out and endangering friendship for the good of the friend
p)   Bond of friendship
q)   Abuse by friends or of friends
r)   Taking friends for granted – failure to appreciate
s)   Not taking friends for granted – appreciating their friendship and them as people
t)   Giving empowerment to friends through your friendship
u)   Being empowered by friends through their friendship
v)   Feeling of belonging
w)   Loss of friendship through ones own actions
x)   Loss of friendship through the actions of another
y)   Grieving for loss of friendship
z)   Anger at loss of freindship

ENVIRONMENTAL LOVE

a)   Love of and respect for the planet

b)   Care of the planet
c)   Care of the environment
d)   Ecological practices
e)   Conservation of species
f)   Conservation of environment
g)   Conservation or management of natural resources
h)   Maintenance, management and preservation of nature
i)   Understanding of or interest in geology, ecology, anthropology, climate, zoology etc
j)   Interest in world affairs
k)   Personal behaviour towards planet and environment
l)   Lack of interest in world affairs
m)   No understanding of or interest in geology, ecology, anthropology, climate, zoology etc
n)   Lack of care of planet or environment
o)   Failure to follow ecological practices
p)   No interest in conservation of species or environment
q)   Rape of natural resources
r)   Being a citizen of Earth

HUMANITARIANISM

a)   Awareness and respect of other cultures
b)   Lack of awareness and respect for the culture of others
c)   Lack of awareness and respect by others for your culture
d)   Care and compassion for all incarnates
e)   Lack of care and compassion for other incarnates
f)   Civilised behaviour towards others
g)   Failure to act in a civilised manner towards others
h)   Failure of others to act in a civilised manner toward you
i)   Charitable behaviour towards others
j)   Failure to be charitable towards others
k)   Failure of others to offer you charitable behaviour
l)   Thoughtfulness and consideration of others
m)   Lack of thoughtfulness and consideration of others
n)   Failure of others to be thoughtful or considerate towards you
o)   Being helpful to others
p)   Being unhelpful to others

q)   Suffering from lack of others help
r)   Being sensitive to others feelings
s)   Lack of sensitivity to others feelings
t)   Others having lack of sensitivity to your feelings
u)   Being a member of the human race
v)   Inhumanity towards others
w)   Abuse of human rights
x)   Upholding human rights
y)   Failure to understand the need for human rights
z)   Having your human rights abused by others
aa) Suffering through ethnic cleansing
bb) Suffering from being ordered to perform ethnic cleansing
cc) Abhorrence of ethnic cleansing
dd) Belief in need for ethnic cleansing
ee) Response to human tragedy
ff) Lack of response to human tragedy

TUTORING

a)   Sharing of knowledge with another
b)   Educate, enlighten and edify another
c)   Being educated, enlightened and edified by another
d)   Failure to share knowledge with another
e)   Acting as a model or example for another
f)   Acting as a bad model or example for another
g)   Following the model or example set by another
h)   Wishing to empower another
i)   Wishing to disempower another
j)   Being disempowered by another
k)   Giving the tools to another to enrich their life
l)   Withholding from another the tools that could enrich their lives
m)   Having the tools withheld by another that could enrich your life
n)   Coaching another to access their strengths and abilities
o)   Disparaging another so that they do not recognise their own strengths and abilities
p)   Being disparaged by another so that you do not recognise your own strengths and abilities

ROMANTIC LOVE

a)   Offering another love and affection
b)   Being offered love and affection by another
c)   Not being offered love and affection by one for whom one feels these emotions
d)   Being tender, warm and caring in one's dealings with a lover
c)   Failing to be tender, warm and caring in one's dealings with a lover
f)   Offering devotion to another
g)   Being offered the devotion of another
h)   Adoration of another
i)   Being adored by another
j)   Passionate and amorous love
k)   Lack of passion in a lover
l)   Doting on another
m)   Being doted on by another
n)   Being demonstrative of one's feelings
o)   Not being able to demonstrate one's feelings
p)   Suffering insecurity because one's lover is unable to demonstrate their feelings
q)   Being idealistic and quixotic
r)   Being preoccupied, wistful, absent minded and completely absorbed in another
s)   Being possessive of another
t)   Being jealous, domineering or controlling
u)   Suffering from the jealousy of a lover
v)   Being domineered or controlled by a lover
w)   Being selfless
x)   Being selfish
y)   Suffering the selfishness of a lover
z)   Being overprotective
aa) Being overprotected
bb) Being reflective and contemplative
cc) Suffering from longing for the object of your love
dd) Separation from the object of your love
ee) Melancholy due to loss of romantic love
ff) Pain from unrequited love

gg)   Insecurity of unrequited love
hh)   Loyalty, lack of loyalty
ii)   Faithfulness or unfaithfulness

LIFE PARTNERSHIP

a)   Union, fusion, bonding
b)   Marriage or form of commitment
c)   Divorce or lack of commitment
d)   Loyalty and faithfulness
e)   Disloyalty and unfaithfulness
f)   Devotion and dedication or lack of
g)   Duty and responsibility or lack of
h)   Companionship
i)   Joining together
j)   Separation
k)   Harmony and accord
l)   Disharmony and discord
m)   Claustrophobia
n)   Feeling of being trapped
o)   Dissatisfaction with partner
p)   Love turning to routine and comfortableness
q)   Growth and deepening of relationship
r)   Growth of understanding of one in close relationship
s)   Learning of behaviour patterns of another
t)   Understanding the behaviour patterns of another
u)   Recognition of another's likes and dislikes
v)   Recognition of another's interests and respect for these even if of no personal interest
w)   Tolerance
x)   Empowerment of another
y)   Pride of another

LOVE OF IDENTITY

a)   Pride in country, region, town, locality, religion, culture or person
b)   Lack of pride in country, region, town, locality, religion, culture or person

c)	Discrimination, intolerance and bigotry of others not of own country, region, town, locality, religion or culture.

d)	Tolerance of others not of own country, region, town, locality, religion or culture

e)	Xenophobia, racism and prejudice

f)	Racial tolerance, globalisation

g)	Love of tradition, ethnicity and customs

h)	Indifference to tradition, ethnicity and custom

i)	Importance of lifestyle and standard of living

j)	Disregard for lifestyle and standard of living

k)	Reluctance to join with other countries in any project

l)	Territorial, protective and defensive

All of these need to be experienced to see that all that matters is to be a citizen of Earth and a spiritual being first and foremost.

SELF-LOVE

a)	Self-love and lack of it

b)	Self-assurance and lack of it

c)	Self-confidence and lack of it

d)	Self-possession and lack of it

e)	Insecurity and uncertainty

f)	Timidity and anxiety

g)	Poise and aplomb

h)	Sang-froid

i)	Composure and lack of it

j)	Self-control and lack of it

k)	Strength of will and lack of it

l)	Strength of mind and lack of it

m)	Restraint and willpower and lack of it

n)	Self-discipline and self-indulgence

o)	Self-esteem and lack of it

p)	Self-belief and lack of it

q)	Self-worth and lack of it

r)	Self-respect and lack of it

s)	Self-image

t)	Personality and character

u)	Honour and dishonour

v)	Respect and disrespect

w)   Reputation
x)   Self-importance and humility
y)   Self-satisfaction and dissatisfaction
z)   Happiness and unhappiness
aa)   Fulfilment and dissatisfaction
bb)   Contentment and discontentment
cc)   Dignity and decorum or lack of it
dd)   Composure and peace of mind or lack of it
ee)   Inner peace or lack of it
ff)   Stress, panic, loss of control
gg)   Fear of life

LOVE OF HOME

a)   Homemaking for self and loved ones
b)   Pride in home
c)   Turning home into status symbol
d)   Realising home is where the heart is
e)   Realising that home is for the comfort it provides and not a yardstick to measure success
f)   Taking pleasure in simple things home can provide
g)   Recognising own space
h)   Having others recognise the need for personal space
i)   Having others respect your personal space
j)   Freedom to be oneself and follow ones own agenda
k)   Duty and routine
l)   Need to maintain the home to show love of it
m)   Neglect of home
n)   Safety, comfort, shelter, sanctuary, refuge, safe-haven, your very own safe place.
o)   The experience of not having any of those things in your home.

LOVE OF PETS

a)   Simply recognising that a pet can be a surrogate child, parent, sibling or friend.
b)   All the emotions of responsibility, care, concern, pain of loss, guilt and joy and happiness that can be generated by a human can be generated by a pet.

c) A pet is unconditional. Many still offer love even if abused or neglected.

d) A pet's role in one's life can be to offer companionship, stability or the one constant in turmoil.

RESPECT

a) Respect has entered many of the above categories but needs a little further explanation of its own.

b) By offering respect to another, one validates them.

c) By disrespecting another, one invalidates them.

GRIEF

a) Anger from grief

b) Anger that you are the one left alone

c) Anger that your life has been turned upside down

d) Anger that things can never again be as they were.

e) Guilt from grief

f) Guilt that you have survived when a loved one has not

g) Guilt at the feeling of relief that can come on the passing of one who has suffered long.

h) Guilt at the fleeting rejoicing at being free from worry over illness of a loved one.

i) Loneliness

j) Sorrow at the grief of another

k) Worry over one consumed by grief

l) Mourning – the prolonged grieving leading to inability to continue with the natural progression of life

m) Heartache so great that it cripples future happiness

n) Dealing with grief by appearing casual or uncaring

o) Failure to understand that a casual, uncaring demeanour can be an indication of inability to deal with grief.

p) The control of grief leading to illness

q) The control of grief leading to mental illness

r) Early death of second partner – heartbreak

s) Regret for things left undone and unsaid

t) Sorrow - sadness caused by the actions of another or oneself – dwelling on matters that cannot be changed.

u)   Anguish – the torment of inconsolable grief, often
      caused by the waiting for the inevitable event to happen
      – the unknown.

v)   Emotional pain – physical symptoms brought on by
      deep grief

w)   Misery – the desolation and wretchedness felt at certain
      situations. The inability to lift out of a depressive or
      melancholy state, or the despair at knowing that one is
      unable to do this with the rational mind, while the
      irrational mind continues its path of destructive gloom.

x)   Unhappiness – general discontent with life, the way a
      path is going, the actions of others. The inability to be
      joyful if not as profound as some of the other elements.

y)   Angst – anxiety, worry, fear – all elements of grief. All
      leading to loss of inner peace.

z)   The witnessing of any or all of these in a loved one,
      which can be harder to bear than being the sufferer.

RELIGION

Again, many lessons in the syllabus to be learned from this
heading. For each positive or negative, the opposite is also
experienced as in all cases. For instance, "superiority practised by
priests over people" – one experience might be as the priest doing
this, one as a priest recognising this and trying not to do so, one as
a member of the priests congregation blindly accepting his
superiority and another as a member questioning his right to act
in this way, and so on. So many ways to experience each aspect.

a)   The foremost aspect of love from this heading is faith
      and belief, both of which are given blindly by religious
      followers in the main.

b)   Trust in religious leaders

c)   Betrayal of trust by religious leaders

d)   Reliance on religion to provide a framework for one's
      life rather than following inner knowledge

e)   Blindly following someone else's vision rather than your
      own

f)   Reliance on the policy of others without understanding
      and question

g)   Disempowering oneself by giving of power to religious representatives

h)   Control! Control! CONTROL!

i)   Dogma and doctrine more important in religion than spirituality

j)   Used as a vehicle for self-advancement of the few

k)   Used by many to obtain feeling of superiority over one's fellow man

l)   Lacking in true love and spirituality

m)   Obsession with the material – churches, trappings ctc

n)   Church uses wealth for self, not for populace

o)   True spirituality has no relationship to religion

p)   Recognition of spiritual truths and that religions are man made.

q)   Recognition that choice or creed is not worth killing each other for as we are all spiritual beings and may reincarnate as a member of the despised religion in our future lives.

r)   Superiority practiced by the priests over the people

GENERAL DESCRIPTION

The word list that follows goes towards showing the many aspects of love, each of which could be used in many of the above categories. The list just indicates the wide range of feelings, actions, thoughts and emotions that are generated by love. It goes without saying that for each description, the opposite needs to be experienced in order to obtain a full understanding.

a)   Admiration

b)   Respect

c)   Esteem

d)   Approbation

e)   High Regard

f)   Appreciation

g)   Approval

h)   Value

i)   Cherish

j)   Hold dear

k)   Have good opinion of

l)   Praise
m)   Have pride in
n)   Like
o)   Support
p)   Bond with
q)   Prop up
r)   Gratitude
s)   Understanding
t)   Compassion
u)   Empathy
v)   Sympathy
w)   Consideration
x)   Thought
y)   Reflection
z)   Selflessness
aa)   Gentleness
bb)   Humanity
cc)   Helpfulness
dd)   Benevolence
ee)   Generosity
ff)   Munificence
gg)   Charitable
hh)   Of importance
ii)   Revere
jj)   Happiness
kk)   Pleasure
ll)   Ecstasy
mm)   Delight
nn)   Contentment
oo)   Care
pp)   Help
qq)   Concern
rr)   Responsibility
ss)   Duty
tt)   Understanding
uu)   Tolerance
vv)   Patience
ww)   Forbearance
xx)   Open-mindedness
yy)   Broad-mindedness

zz)   Empowerment

And so on...................................

This is only the tip of a very large iceberg!

What life means for you in particular at the present time is what experiences from the list you wrote in your life-plan with the intention to complete this time. Some experiences repeat, depending on one's spiritual age. We have a saying; "the older you are spiritually, the more difficult will be the life". If your life has been one of unbroken hardship and struggle, the explanation might be that you are at the "university" stage of the spiritual journey. What is true also, is that all spirit must experience everything. Those that have a seemingly gilded life with little trauma will in due course, experience the opposite, or may have done so previously. The definition of a spiritual master is one who has experienced everything. All of us will become masters eventually. We are each a part of a greater whole, on a journey of evolving our soul at the end of which we return to enrich the Source, as bees to a hive.

SOME WAYS TO USE THIS

In answer to the question, what am I here for? a first step might be to read this list and see if any bells ring concerning events in life so far. If they have rung, then there may be comfort in knowing both that they were intended, and not chance, and secondly through experience of them, you will have advanced along the spiritual journey.

For those who are familiar and comfortable with the technique of pendulum dowsing, you may be able to put questions to your guide about your life purpose. I must advise firstly that all answers are at the discretion of the guide, and secondly be very careful how you frame the question. It is only the actual question asked, not the thought you had, that will be answered in that way. Questions about third parties will not usually be answered.

In general a guide will not reveal in advance what the life plan is.

There are exceptions however, when for example, a guide will confirm a path once a person has made a key decision to go along it. What a guide will not do is make decisions for us. It is for us to discover our destiny, but the guide will give us nudges and prompts to assist. Some questions one might put include:

i)   Am I on track with my life plan?
ii)   Have I experienced my major plot yet?
iii)   Have I met my soul-mate yet?
iv)   Have I known X in a past life?
v)   Was it one, two, or many times? (Three questions).
vi)   Is X a member of my soul-group?
vii)   Was X an intended event in my life-plan?
viii)   Was X a scripted event in my life-plan?
ix)   Was X a "wrong time, wrong place" scenario?
x)   Was X for the spiritual growth of another, not primarily for me?
xi)   Am I a young, middle age or old spirit? (Three questions).
xii)   Am I on a repeat life?
xiii)   If so, is it because I have difficulty with X?
xiv)   Did I meet X because it was spirit arranged?
xv)   Was X an unintended event in my life plan?
xvi)   Is Earth my planet of origin?
xvii)   Do I have a special task to perform in relation to the ascension?
xviii) Is my life task centred on healing, counselling, mediumship, earth energies, teaching, other? (Six questions).

As we approach 2012, and in the years beyond it, more and more people are going to find they have spirit communication. The best use of a pendulum is for confirmation of a thought or feeling. If you require more than that, then mediumship may be appropriate. If so one will often feel a prompt to do so, and actual choice of the particular medium will usually be guide assisted as well.

Please note, these questions will only be answered "yes", "no" or "no answer." The answer may require consideration of a number of aspects, pro's and con's, so do exercise caution and do not rely exclusively on a pendulum answer if it involves an important change in your life. Also be aware that a guide may answer spiritually (i.e. what is correct for your life-plan.) You may be asking on a human level, which may require a different answer. Please remember also, everything is subject to free-will choice and the free-will choices of others. These can sometimes delay if not derail life-plans.

I discussed some of the ways in which a life-plan is written in my book *"Why Come Back? Book Two"*. One thing not included there is the fact, each life-plan will have seven levels contained within it. In chapter four I used my own plan as an illustration of odd numbers, the self-employment phase of eighteen years was one such level of my own plan.

In my case, my levels were these which I use as an example:

	Level	No of years
Birth to eighteen – childhood and schooling.	1	18
18-21 – should have been university, but through choice did not go	2	3
21-32 – employment	3	11
33-50 – self-employment	4	18
50-55 – spiritual philosopher and writer	5	5
55-70 – teacher of spiritual philosophy	6	15
70+ – retirement	7	2

There are three strands in a life-plan running simultaneously. The above list is the main one of occupation or principal activity. There are also "spirituality" and "relationship" strands. The three do not necessarily coincide with each other. Spirituality and relationships can have, and mostly do, have less than seven levels. A change in level of "relationship" does not necessarily mean a new partner, but a change in how that relationship exists for example.

Although written into the plan, I have left out date of death or life end transition, as blank because various scenarios are written in the plan in my own case. Depending on the choices made by others, my old age may be brief or long, two years or twenty. I wrote earlier that the approximate time of one's death will be in the life-plan. That is true for the vast majority of cases, I am one of the exceptions. Please note also that a guide may not confirm longevity, depending on whether it is something you do not need to know. One of the abilities mankind will have in the future is the means to determine life-span. That will be at a time when spiritual truths are so well known they are taken as read. A future equivalent of Cardinal Newman, will then here be reminding us, have we fully experienced all we planned to do before we decide to return back to spirit?

ABOUT THE AUTHOR

Roger Burman had very much a conventional material life until aged forty-nine. That was one of a professional career, a self-employed accountant, a family and three children, a divorce. He gave up his business, home and possessions to take on a more spiritual life-style. This was living on board a converted wooden fishing boat. There he has written his four books to date.

He met his partner Angie in January 2000 until March 2007. She had first rate mediumship skills through which Roger initially obtained his philosophy from spirit. Over time Roger has developed his own communication abilities.

Roger has specialism in research and teaching about the planet's own energies, referred to in this book.

BOOKS BY THE SAME AUTHOR

"Why Come Back?" ISBN 9780954204709

We each have a life-plan, the book describes what they are, how they are formulated, what goes into them, how they are the yardstick for review on return to spirit. The book describes what "spiritual growth" is, the object of life-plan, which ultimately is to experience the multi-faceted nature of "unconditional love".

The book's unique contribution to greater spiritual knowledge is the introduction of the concept of the Spiritual Three, awareness of which is fundamental to learning about spirit and the spiritual journey.

Price £10.99

"Why Come Back? Book Two" ISBN 9780954204716

This gives illustrations and examples of many incarnations of the soul including the spiritual perspective behind the painful human experiences, and spiritual explanations for the times themselves, using the author's own past lives, supplemented by mediumship enquiries.

More detail is revealed about spirit guides, Spirit Council, spirit and time, how the future is known, what fairies are, animal spirit and much more.

The rare quality of the author's communication is movingly demonstrated with examples of "spirit letters" of personal messages from spirit, to loved ones on the earth plane.

Price £10.99

BOOKS BY THE SAME AUTHOR

"Nothing Happens by Accident" ISBN 9780954204723

Further information and examples of the spirit three is given. The unfolding of life-plan is illustrated by the example of ten famous Britons. The influence of past lives on the present one is discussed. Why we attract the disease we need by discussing illness from the spiritual perspective. The over-arching spiritual orchestration that accompanies all life is shown.

Price £10.99

The first three books above are a trilogy to explain life-plan, reincarnation, and spiritual journey.